Curiosities from Scarborough's Children's Charities

Scarborough Castle, Yorkshire. DUGDALE 1845 old antique print

Anne Morley

Copyright © Anne Morley 2017

All rights reserved. No part of this publication may be reproduced, stored in a retrieval system, or transmitted, in any form or by any means, electronic, mechanical, photocopying, recording or otherwise, without the prior permission of both the copyright owner and the publisher.

Anne Morley has asserted her right to be identified as the author of this work in accordance with the Copyright, Designs and Patents Act 1988.

If you are a copyright holder and feel your contribution has not been acknowledged, please advise the publisher and an acknowledgement will be placed in any future edition.

First published in Great Britain in 2017
by
Farthings Publishing
8 Christine House
Scarborough YO11 2QB
UK

http://www.farthings-publishing.com

ISBN 978-0-244-01353-0

August 2017 (f)

Contents

	Acknowledgements	viii
	Foreword	xiii
PART ONE	The Grammar School Trust	15
	• Connections with St Mary's Church	
	• The Civil Wars	
	• The Farrars and the Spa	
	• The Grammar School relocates	
	• The Arrival of the Railway	
	• The Rowntree Family	
	• St Martin's Grammar School	
	• The New Grammar Schools	
PART TWO	Falsgrave Town Trust	34
	• Tostig's legacy	
	• The Franciscan Friars	
	• Falsgrave Endowed School	
	• The Township of Falsgrave	
	• Resistance to Change	
PART THREE	Acts and Influences	53
	• A Changing Society	
	• 1835 Municipal Corporations Reform Act	
	• Forster's Education Act	
	• Scarborough School Board	
	• William Ascough in Burnley	
	• James Kay-Shuttleworth, Educationalist	
	• William Ascough in Derbyshire	
	• The Sitwell Family	
	• William Ascough and the Scarborough School Board	
	• The Balgarnies	
	• More Board Schools	
	• Scarborough School of Art	
	• The Muni	

- The University Extension Society and Sir Arthur Herbert Dyke Acland
- Education Act 1902
- Moving on

PART FOUR   Scarborough United Scholarships Foundation   83
- The Scheme of 1888
- Scarborough School Board Scholarships and Prizes
- The Whittaker Family
- SUSF amalgamates with the Amicable Society
- The Mechanics Institute
- Added extras: *The Glauert Mathematics Prize; The Scarborough Schools Prize Fund; The Taylor Education Fund; The Nessie Linn Memorial Trust Fund*
- The Graham Family
- Distribution of funds in 1921 and 1922 and some consequences

PART FIVE   Scarborough Amicable Society   117
- Robert North
- The First Amicable Schools
- Celebrations in 1860
- A New School for the Amicable Society
- New Rules and Regulations
- The Cock Hill Close Trust
- Closure of the Schools
- Seeking a New Role
- After the Amalgamation
- Diversification
- 'Reversion to the Old Order of Things'
- 250 years on
- The Park Lodge Charity

PART SIX   People connected with the Amicable Society   170
- Henrietta Griffiths
- The Mosey Family
- Charlotte Morley
- Archdeacon Richard Frederick Lefevre Blunt

- John Richard Halliday
- Octavia Flora Morgan
- George Lord Beeforth
- Simpson Parkinson
- William Tindall
- John Jackson
- Ernest Trott
- The Forty Club

PART SEVEN The John Kendall Trust   197
- The Charity in 1941
- The earlier years
- The Alice Brooke Home
- From 1980
- Colonel John Kendall
- The Woodalls
- Reverend Frederick Kendall
- The Spofforth Connection
- Rear Admiral John Kendall

In Conclusion   234

Acknowledgements

The original minute books from all three charities were great source material. Although the first hundred years of the Amicable Society is missing, many references to the early years are to be found in the Annual Reports and other documents discovered in the tin trunks. The first six volumes were particularly useful: 1835 – 1863, 1889 – 1897, 1898 – 1903, 1904 – 1921, 1921 – 1931 and 1932 – 1952.

The first volume of SUSF Minutes was located in Scarborough Library together with the deeds of sale of the Falsgrave Town fields. The second volume, September 1928 to September 2000, and the John Kendall Trust Minutes, from February 1942 to January 2005, had been handed to me on taking over as Secretary.

The wonders of modern technology have helped enormously. David Moore kindly sent the digitised version of all the Scarborough School Board Minutes and the Scarborough Education Committee Minutes up to 1926 along with the early Forty Club Minutes, so I could peruse them at my leisure. Thanks to The Genealogist, a family history research site, I was able to delve into people's history then check further on Google where I discovered all sorts of bits and pieces.

One of these was Thomas Hinderwell's 'History and Antiquities of the Vicinity of Scarborough' first published in 1811. Another was 'Cole's Scarborough Guide' of 1824 from John Cole's library, followed by 'Theakston's Guide to Scarborough' written by Solomon Wilkinson Theakston and first published in 1840. A compilation from the Scarborough Gazette in 1901 entitled 'Some Scarborough Faces' proved very useful. The Rowntree Society has placed the history of both the York and the Scarborough branches of this family on the internet, I particularly thank them for 'The Genealogy of the

Rowntrees of Risborough' compiled by Charles Brigwen Rowntree.

Again it was through Google I found George Alfred Raikes' 'Historical Records of the First Regiment of Third West York Light Infantry', Frederick Kendall's 'Catalogue of the Minerals and Fossils of Scarborough', Peter C Robinson's 'Early Scarborough Geologists' and H S Torrens' 'Scarborough's First Geologists' that revealed so much of interest about John Kendall's ancestry. An email contact through the museum to Jim Middleton, who happened to be researching the same subject matter, brought more details.

Specialist information came from Trish McNaughton, Church Historian at St Andrew's Unitarian Church, known to the locals as 'Balgarnie's' and Revd R Balgarnie's book 'Sir Titus Salt'. 'The Journal of the Swinnerton Society Volume 11' helped locate a gentleman I had had great difficulty finding. James Bantoft was a well respected authority on the Sitwells, I found a copy of 'The Sitwells in Scarborough' from November 2008, that he had prepared for the Sitwell Society and heard him give a talk on the subject.

I discovered Charles William Sutton's 1891 article on Sir James Phillips Kay-Shuttleworth (1804 – 1877) and from the House of Commons Parliamentary Papers on line came authentic information in 'Reports on Elementary Schools General Report 1879 by HMI T S Aldis' on the schools he inspected in the Harrogate District of Yorkshire. I am grateful to Frank Green, a past committee member, for his 1974 booklet 'Scarborough Amicable Society, a Historical Sketch' and similarly L Pickard for his 'Scarborough United Scholarships Foundation, a brief history' written in 1980. I thank another member of the Amicable Society and Church Warden at the Parish Church, Maurice Horspool, for his 1991 booklet 'The Stones of St Mary's Scarborough', the Church website was informative too.

The Scarborough Girls' High School Old Girls' Association provided much background to Miss Glauert and the original Girls' High School from their website and copies of newspaper articles. For personal reminiscences I thank both Hilary Watts, on his grandfather, Revd Watts, Sydney McCloy and Frances Spofforth and also Dena Hebditch when I was trying to locate Nessie Linn and the Park House Trustees.

I thank David Sutcliffe for his encouragement and for locating the photograph of the Amicable schoolboys. Another source was David Fowler, I thank him for publishing the Boys' High School 'Summer Times' magazine, a source of information on 'The Muni' and the grammar schools. Now I thank him for agreeing to publish my efforts and for all his care and encouragement.

Many general references were gleaned through GENUKI (UK and Ireland Genealogy) and old Scarborough Gazetteers and Directories on line. Local information came from the Scarborough Maritime Heritage both on line and visiting, the Scarborough Archaeological Society discoveries, especially with reference to Falsgrave, and my husband John Morley whose College Thesis in 1959 was on 'The History of Education in Scarborough' documenting the Amicable Society schools and those of the School Board.

Finally to Jack Binns, the ultimate authority on Scarborough's history, I thank him for sharing his vast knowledge through his books, articles in the Scarborough News and various talks he has given. I should mention two of his books particularly 'A place of Great Importance, Scarborough in the Civil Wars' (1996) and 'The History of Scarborough North Yorkshire' (2001).

I have mentioned my contact in Australia, David Moore, whom I have now met. I thank him for sharing his own research into the Ascough Family as well as the digitised Minute Books and above all for his and Gillian's friendship.

Ainsworth's Scarborough Guide 1844
Revd R Balgarnie 'Sir Titus Salt'.
James Bantoft 'The Sitwells in Scarborough'
Henri Bencker 'Chronological list of the main maritime discoveries and explorations' printed in August 1944 in the International Hydrographic Review

Jack Binns 'A place of Great Importance, Scarborough in the Civil Wars' (1996)
Jack Binns 'The History of Scarborough North Yorkshire' (2001).
G Broadrick 'New Scarborough Guide' (1811)
John Cole, 'Graphical and historical Sketches of Scarborough' 1824
John Cole 'Scarborough Repository and Mirror of the Season, Volume 1' 1824,
Elizabeth Crawford 'The Women's Suffrage Movement'
Fairford History Society Newsletter January 2013 article on John Swalwell
Anthony Faulkes, 'Story of Heming'
David Fowler 'Scarborough Snippets'
'Summer Times' The Journal of the Old Scarborians, published by David Fowler, including
'THE WESTWOOD SCHOOL AT SCARBOROUGH 1902-1952' by the late HW Marsden
Frank Green 'Scarborough Amicable Society, a Historical Sketch' 1987
John Grimshaw's philatelic article on St Helena
Thomas Hinderwell 'History and Antiquities of the Vicinity of Scarborough' published 1811
Robert Hornsey 'Visitant's Guide' (c1835)
Maurice Horspool, 'The Stones of St Mary's Scarborough'1991
Frederick Kendall's 'Catalogue of the Minerals and Fossils of Scarborough'
Warren Bert Kimberley 'The History of West Australia'
Charles Knight, London 1834 publisher 'The Printing Machine'
NUT Easter 1906 Conference Guide and Souvenir (A E Morley's copy)
L Pickard 'Scarborough United Scholarships Foundation, a brief history' 1980
G A Raikes' 'Historical Records of the First Regiment of Third West York Light Infantry',
Peter C Robinson's 'Early Scarborough Geologists'
Charles Brigwen Rowntree 'The Genealogy of the Rowntrees of Risborough'

Owen Rutter 'British North Borneo'. (1922)
Scarborough Museums Trust, Cover photo of painting of The Crown Tavern, (Bleach House) Scarborough. Artist unknown.
Captain Ralph Spofforth 'A New History of the Spofforth Family'
Snorri Sturleson's Icelandic saga
Charles William Sutton's 1891 'Sir James Phillips Kay-Shuttleworth (1804 – 1877)'
Solomon Wilkinson Theakston 'Guide to Scarborough'+
H S Torrens' 'Scarborough's First Geologists'
John Venn 'Alumni Cantabrigienses'
Stephen Whatley's Gazetteer of 1750
'Wells of Yorkshire' family history website re William Hewitt

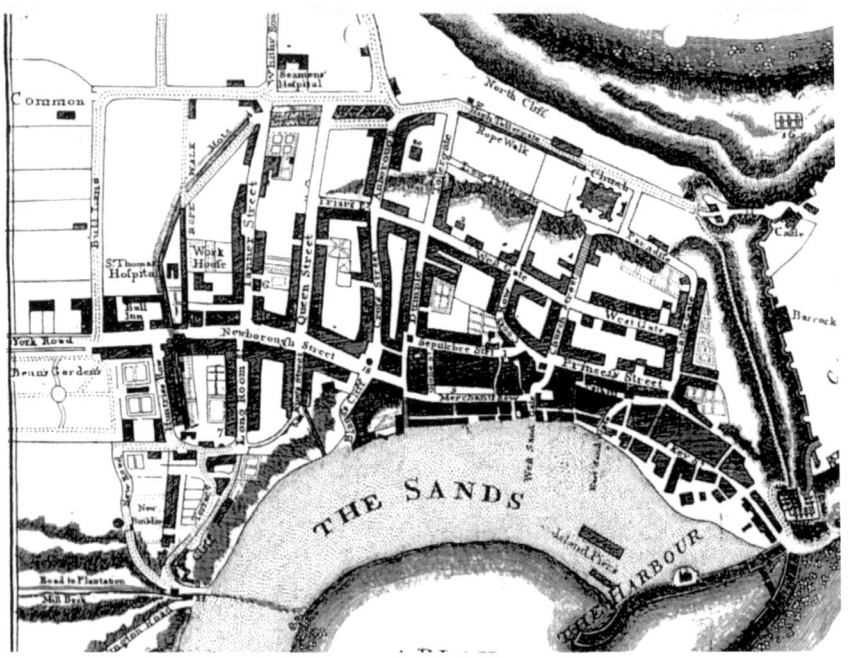

An early map of Scarborough

Foreword

A few years ago I began to look into the whys and wherefores of the Children's Charities in Scarborough but when two tin trunks labelled 'Scarborough Amicable Society' were dumped at our house I was hooked. Their hidden treasure was too precious to confine to some repository without first blowing the dust off the old Minute Books and allied documents to investigate a forgotten realm.

My husband, John, had been the NUT representative on the Amicable Society Committee since 1968, he took over as Secretary in September 2003. I had been on the Scarborough United Scholarships Foundation and the John Kendall Trust as a representative from St Mary's Church since 1994 and was appointed Secretary in May 2003. I simply had to delve in and discover more about these wonderful charities.

Incentive number two came when I was given what turned out to be a pivotal contact. In Australia David Moore was researching connections in Scarborough for his family history. These included Gladstone Road School, where John taught, as had his Father and Grandfather I discovered. Thanks to David, we have detailed knowledge of his great-grandfather, William Ascough, Clerk to the Scarborough School Board no less and Secretary of the Amicable Society. Until then he had simply been a name in the minute books.

Entwined in their history are so many curious stories - come exploring with me around the streets of Scarborough and beyond through the passage of time. Some of the characters we meet are already well documented, others entirely forgotten but they all played a part in the formation of these charities. Through their exploits we will reveal something of the way life has developed.

Like David and John, you might find someone from your family in these pages.

PART ONE
The Grammar School Trust

Connections with St Mary's Church

Richard Lionheart was waiting in Dover on 11 December 1189, about to set off on his Crusade, when he donated the tithes of St Mary's Church in Scarborough to the Cistercians. Why? Rather than take the longer, choppier voyage by sea to join the rest of the Crusade in the Mediterranean, he could cross France and stay in the relative comfort of the Cistercian monasteries en route. The forfeiture of these tithes *'especially of a fishing called Doguedrave'* (probably fish caught on the Dogger Bank) was to be given *'in pure and perpetual alms ... for the abbots at the time of the general chapter'*.

No doubt the monks feasted well when they met every three years for their Chapter Meetings in Cîteaux, unfortunately it was at the expense of the people of Scarborough who had to forego a tenth of the income from all the cod, codfish oil and herring caught for the next two hundred years. It has been suggested that the white-habited Cistercian monks may have lived in a mansion with an enclosed garden near the church, namely 'Paradise'.

As a monastic institution (it was never a monastery) we can assume the monks would have had a Grammar School at St Mary's. The first written evidence of this comes on 12 July 1457 when Richard Wardale, Burgess in the Common Hall, asked to be buried *'near the font where Hugo Rasen, formerly Grammar School Master, was buried'*. Mr Rasen was an acclaimed teacher, the Grammar School in Hull wished to employ him when they had a vacancy in 1444 but he stayed in Scarborough. Thomas Hinderwell includes

'Hugo Raysyn' in his list of Scarborough MPs in 1422 in the new Parliament of Henry IV together with Will Forester.

The Common Hall was situated in Quay Street and served a similar purpose to that of the present day Town Hall. The system had been set up under Henry III in 1356 and lasted until 1835; it consisted of 44 men and was divided into three sets of twelve persons. On 30 September, known as both Michaelmas Day and St Jerome's Day, they elected two of their members as senior and junior bailiffs who acted as justices of the peace and judges at the Court of Pleas; the following year they became coroners. The Common Hall was responsible for the running of the town, it was a self-perpetuating body, selected by and drawn from the same families and consequently not liked by the general inhabitants.

Under Henry IV, the tithes were cancelled and the church together with its revenues was transferred to the custody of the Augustinian Black Canons of the Priory in Bridlington. Less than 150 years later came Henry VIII's Dissolution of the Monasteries when all churches were made Protestant and control passed to the crown. The Grammar School was housed in the Charnel Garth in a chapel that had been founded in 1394 by Sir Robert Percehay of Ryton.

We know of two further teachers at the school, one Henry Langdale, Vicar, taught from 1559 to 1597 almost the full length of Elizabeth 1's reign. Dr Binns informs us of this new Protestant vicar's credentials:

> '...four years as an undergraduate at St Benedict's, later Corpus Christi College, Cambridge. Later he had been assistant at that university to the professor of Greek. When examined for his competence to teach he had excelled in Latin. His testimonial approved at York in 1563 ended by saying that he had licence to teach grammar to boys anywhere in the archdiocese.'

Gregory Dickinson, took over until 1626 when there were around 20 boys each paying an annual fee of 10 shillings. The scholars, who had to be literate and numerate before joining the school, would be taught Latin and Greek.

The first charitable bequest came in 1640 when Gregory Fysh, a bailiff of the town, bequeathed:

'...unto the grammar school where it is now, or shall be, within the liberties of Scarborough, one close with the appurtenances, lying in Worlington Grove ... there shall be four poor scholars continually kept.'

Here we have the foundation of the Grammar School Trust, land in Upper Ramsdale that later became known as 'Grammar School Field'.

The Civil Wars

Charles I raised taxes, fought the Scots and dissolved Parliament then Civil War broke out in 1642. Sir Hugh Cholmley, burgess and Governor of Scarborough Castle, was originally a Parliamentarian but changed sides. As a Royalist, he promised there would be no fighting in the streets so he led his troops into the castle. He had not bargained for the likes of Sir John Meldrum who persuaded his Parliamentarian masters in London that the sea-port of Scarborough was of strategic significance. He selected St Mary's church as his stronghold and had *'the best battering piece'* brought from York. This was a royal-cannon that weighed three and a half tons and was pulled by eight pairs of horses. It could fire 65 pound (29kg) cannonballs and was placed in the chancel of the church.

The Parliamentarians succeeded in demolishing the west wall of the castle keep as well as the east transept of the church. Cholmley surrendered some weeks later mainly because he and his men were suffering with scurvy. Meldrum, aged over 70, attacked the castle by climbing up the cliff face; he was blown off, fell *'att least steeple height'* and was unconscious for three days. He recovered but during hand to hand fighting took a fatal musket ball *'in att the bellie and out of the backe'*. Colonel Boynton, who took over the Parliamentarians after Meldrum's death, held the Castle in the intervening period whilst his soldiers were billeted in the town.

In the shorter Second Siege, however, as the Parliamentarians failed to pay them, history repeated itself and Boynton turned Royalist, declaring for the imprisoned King Charles by draping a red flag over the castle wall on 27 July 1648. A paper in the archives reads:

> *'The ancient Grammar School, previously conducted in or near the premises of the chapel of St Mary Magdalene in Charnel Garth, was re-housed by order of the Corporation dated 14th February 1648, in the south transept of St Mary's.*
>
> *The Parliamentary commander had given notice that he intended demolishing the Charnel Garth buildings to improve his line of fire in besieging the Castle.*
>
> *In this year, 1648, Francis Thompson, a senior bailiff of the town, gave to the Corporation £100 in trust for the income thereof, £5 p. a., to be paid to the Vicar of St. Mary's and entered in the Corporation books 'for the use of the school''.*

This too was further income to be inherited by the Trust.

Francis Thompson became MP for Scarborough under Charles II, James II and William III. The Corporation's order was carried out and the Grammar School moved into 'temporary' accommodation in Farrar's Aisle, the south transept of St Mary's Church, where it remained for the next two hundred years. Apparently Colonel Boynton removed the stones from the Charnel Garth and used them to block off the school from the main church; a doorway was made in the west wall for the boys to use.

St Mary's Church showing the South Transept where the Grammar School was housed

The castle similarly was no longer the building it had been but it continued to serve as a barracks and a prison under its Parliamentarian Governor, Colonel Bethell. Perhaps its most famous prisoner was George Fox, founder of the Quakers who spent a miserable time there from April 1665 until September 1666. However, when visiting the area after his release, George Fox accepted an invitation from Jordan Croslands, who had become Governor of Scarborough Castle. Apparently he was received *'very courteously and lovingly'*.

Throughout this troubled period Mr William Penston was the headmaster of the school; having taken up the post in 1627 he retired in 1677 by which time he had become both deaf and blind. The school had 30 to 40 scholars, most likely many were the sons of the burgesses; at this time we are told each scholar was expected to know the alphabet before admission. Revd Henry Docker followed Mr Penston, he became Vicar of St Mary's in 1708, following the death of Revd John North.

The Farrars and the Spa

Farrar's Aisle, home to the Grammar School, was named after John Farrer, burgess, property owner, a leading ship-owner and another example of the inter-relationships amongst the town's ruling classes. In 1600 he had married Thomasine Hutchinson of Wykeham Abbey, whose sister Isabel was married to Christopher Thompson, son of William and brother of Francis Thompson MP. William was half-brother to William Fysh and was also Warden of the Scarborough Shipowners' Company. John Farrer was one of the nine people involved in Scarborough's salt making businesses. The burgesses monopolised the town's businesses as they also controlled the refining of train oil.

This smelly trade of rendering oil from whale and seal blubber for use in machinery took place on what we now call St Nicholas Cliff, while salt was obtained by boiling down sea water on the south sands. Both were lucrative operations, only accessible to the rich as they required expensive equipment and a lot of sea coal. At this time Scarborough consisted of some 450 households and about 30 ships, mainly trading in Tyneside coal, Yorkshire cloth and landing fish, wine, grain and spices. The burgesses in the Common Hall were responsible for the upkeep of the harbour and piers as well as the water supply and the behaviour of the inhabitants.

John Farrer was a bailiff in 1602 and again in 1625, Christopher Thompson held the position in 1604, 1610 and 1617 and William Thompson in 1605, 1611 and 1620. Thomasine's brother, Stephen Hutchinson, followed William Thompson as the second MP for Scarborough in 1626 with

Sir Hugh Cholmley as first MP both years. Shortly before his death in 1628, John Farrer bequeathed two tenements as a charity home for two poor widows in Cook's Row, near Low Conduit. This must have entitled him to recognition with a memorial in St Mary's Church thus giving his name to the South Aisle.

Scarborough owes much to his wife, Thomasine Farrer, for its success as a holiday resort. While she was walking in the South Bay around 1626 she noticed that the water from a spring had turned the rocks a strange colour. Her keen observation had to wait until after the Civil War for Dr Robert Wittie to exploit this phenomenon and thus began Scarborough's tourist industry. Wittie's booklet 'Scarborough Spaw' published in 1660, advised the gentry to cure all their ills by drinking the spa water at source and bathing in the sea; he also advertised in the 'Parliamentary Intelligencer' and 'Mercurius Publicus' in London. Perhaps his connection with Sir Hugh Cholmley helped his cause, they had attended Beverley Grammar School together.

The Assembly at Scarborough by Rowlandson, fitting Daniel Defoe's description of the Long Room

Daniel Defoe visited the town in 1727 and found *'a good deal of company'*. The Long Room was where the Town Hall now stands and gave its name 'Long Room Street' to what is now known as St Nicholas Street. It was described as:

'a noble and spacious building with a view for leagues over the sea'. Balls were held there every evening in the season 'when the Room is illuminated like a Court Assembly'.

To give some idea as to what this spring was like, Stephen Whatley's Gazetteer of 1750 describes it as:

'purgative and diuretic ... and yields 24 gallons of water in an hour. Its qualities are a compound of vitriol, iron, allom, nitre and salt; and it is very transparent, something like a sky colour. It has a pleasant taste from the vitriol and an inky smell.'

Dicky Dickinson gave himself the title of Governor of the Spa and built premises, including toilets, on land he rented from the Corporation.

Beside the sea in Scarborough in 1776

We are told that *'Chairs from London plied in the principal streets'* and the visitors, or 'Spaws' as they were nicknamed, were fed at the New Inn, the New Globe, the Blacksmith's Arms, the Crown and Sceptre and the Old Globe.

The spa building eventually housed Henry Wyatt's Gothic Saloon, a concert hall, in 1826. Soon after, the Cliff Bridge Company had made it more accessible from the town by constructing the Cliff Bridge. St Mary's church had also undergone transformations. The sieges had shaken the foundations and as a result the central tower collapsed in 1659, it was replaced in 1669. Originally there had been twin towers with pyramid roofs at the west end but they had been removed in the 14th century. We note that in the 1700s, Tristram Fysh Esq paid for some pews to be erected in the west gallery of the church *'for the use of the boys and girls of the charity school'*; these were the pupils attending the Amicable Society's Schools. Worshippers at St Mary's paid to use the 600 boxed pews scattered at various levels round the church, the nearer the front the higher the price. It was customary for this revenue to be used to pay the vicar.

Stephen Whatley tells us more about the thriving town in 1750: it had one of the best harbours, ships plying between Newcastle and the Humber could shelter; the pier was maintained from the duty paid on coal from Newcastle and Sunderland; fishermen caught and landed mackerel, turbot, cod and a variety of other fish to supply towns in Yorkshire. There was also a good trade which they shared with the Dutch fishing fleet in drying and salting fish.

The Grammar School relocates

In 1824, whilst Revd John Kirk was Vicar of St Mary's, the forerunners of the Charity Commission looked into the misappropriation by the town council of the income from Gregory Fysh's legacy; the Charity Commission as we know it was not established until 1853. It ruled that the school was not the prerogative of the church, even though it was still housed in Farrar's Aisle. As a result, the council appointed a schoolteacher on £5 per annum to teach Arithmetic and English, a change from the Greek and Latin of Fysh's time, to four poor scholars. These commissioners deemed Thomas Irvin, Curate of St Mary's for 40 years, a very able teacher, who had broadened the curriculum to suit the 40 fee paying boys. Some of these scholars would have had aspirations to go to university and take up professions whilst others would become farmers and traders. Some pupils boarded with Irvin at his house in Queen Street.

Thomas Irvine retired in 1833 and Revd Joseph Skelton, the last Anglican clergyman to run the school, became the master in 1834. William Merry took over in 1838 and ten years later the new vicar of St Mary's, Revd John Whiteside, closed the church for two years while a complete renovation took place. This was a thorough job that included the removal of the proliferation of pews, the new church held only 400 pews. Services in the interim were held in Christ Church, officially a 'chapel of ease', which had been opened in 1828 in Vernon Road to accommodate the vast number of visitors. It seems to have been a popular decision as a memorial window 'the gift of friends' was dedicated to Revd Whiteside when Christ Church was renovated.

So what happened to the Grammar School? It had moved into a different part of the church before the renovation, Farrer's Aisle had become the choir vestry and the standard of education had deteriorated. From the time of the renovation, the laymen who took on the position of Headmaster had to find their own premises. William Merry, who lived at 5 King Street, requested money from the Town Council to erect a new schoolroom but was refused. He ran the school in his own house until 1852 when James Sykes took over until 1861 from premises in York Place. We have a first-hand account from Joshua Rowntree of that renowned Quaker family, who later became an MP for Scarborough. Writing about his time at the school in York Place:

> *"At the age of eight I went to the Scarborough grammar school, kept by a clergyman. He believed much in dunce-caps and in caning. I have seen five boys whacked and perched up at once. My recollection of the religious teaching is very unedifying. Within a year I was withdrawn."*

Mr Sykes was not a clergyman but the rest holds true, by the time he gave up the school there were only four pupils remaining.

From 1861 to 1872 John Swalwell ran the school from a rented room in St Thomas Street. The number of pupils increased to 75, the curriculum included Classics, Mathematics, Latin, Greek, French and German and he rented a nearby field for games. Some boys from as far away as Gloucestershire and Somerset boarded at his house. There were three classes and pupils could only progress into the next class if they had performed well in the half-yearly examinations.

Born in Allerston in 1829, the son of an agricultural labourer, John Swalwell enrolled at St Catharine's College, Cambridge in 1865, paying his own tuition fees. He graduated in 1869 and was ordained a priest, taking up an appointment as Curate in Ebberston the same year. It would appear that he continued as Head of the school whilst pursuing his university studies and some years later whilst he was Vicar of Sinnington, he also held the post of Headmaster at Pickering Grammar School.

The Arrival of the Railway

Scarborough was growing rapidly with an influx of upper class residents particularly on the developing South Cliff. An innovation that had impact on both the town and the

Grammar School Trust was the arrival of the railway with the grand opening of the not-quite-completed station on 7 July 1845.

The day had been declared a Public Holiday in Scarborough so when the train with its 35 carriages pulled into the station there were some ten thousand spectators waiting to greet it. The journey had taken three hours, which included celebratory stops along the way. Lunch for the great and the good, including George Hudson himself, three times Lord Mayor of York and dealer in railway companies, was served under a temporary roof. The Mayor of Scarborough proposed a toast to *'that King of Railway Directors – George Hudson.'* The town was now accessible to day trippers, a different species from the genteel families who could afford to come by carriage and stay for weeks at a time.

Before the line could be laid, land had been purchased between York and Scarborough; among the assets sold by Scarborough Corporation was the Grammar School Field. When the Improvement Commissioners, a body that had been formed by an Act of Parliament in 1805, looked into this, they ordered the Borough Treasurer to return £150 to the Grammar School Trustees, Messrs Bean and Wellburn. It took until 1851 for the money to be handed over. Could the Rowntree Family have been instrumental in uncovering the irregularity?

The Rowntree Family

This influential family originated as farmers at Risborough near Pickering. William Rowntree married Hannah Hebron, both were Quakers, they had five sons and four daughters. Their son, John, born in Risborough in 1757, was already apprenticed to a draper in Scarborough when he married Elizabeth Lotherington in 1785. The Lotheringtons were also Quakers, in the ship-owning business; Elizabeth's father was a sea captain and it is possible her husband had been a sea captain too. They settled at 11 Princess Street where they had three sons and four daughters.

John, their middle son, born in 1789, went to the Quaker school, Ackworth, as a boarder; on leaving he returned to work in the family grocery business in Scarborough. He married Jane Priestman and they had five children. He died in 1845 but the business continued. It was their son Joshua, born in 1844, who had attended Syke's school before moving to Bootham Quaker School in York. He trained as a solicitor in London and York before joining Drawbridge's in Scarborough. He was Mayor of Scarborough from 1885 to 1886 then he became Scarborough's MP as a Gladstonian Liberal from 1886 to 1892. Later he sat on the Education Committee.

John's younger brother Joseph, born in 1801, moved to York where his son, also Joseph, founded the renowned cocoa and chocolate business and many charitable trusts. The family had not been able to afford to send Joseph to Ackworth so he had left school at 13 to work in the grocer's shop which was then on the corner of Bland's Cliff and Cross Street. This was where, helped by his brothers and sisters, he learned how to run a business, developing a facility for figures.

On reaching his 21st birthday, Joseph bought premises on Pavement in York and set up his grocery shop which also dealt in tea and coffee. Joseph's middle son, Joseph, together with his younger brother Henry, began the famous York cocoa business in 1869. Father Joseph took an interest in local politics in York, keeping to his scrupulous moral principles. He was very involved in education, particularly with the Quaker Schools, Bootham, The Mount and Ackworth School. He still found figures and statistics particularly interesting so perhaps that is why, after George Hudson's dealings were exposed in 1849, he was asked to look into the irregularities of the York and North Midland Railway Company.

Joseph Rowntree had bought shares in the company that built the line to Scarborough even though Hudson's vagueness relating to the actual cost of his projects worried him. Did he discover the sale of the Grammar School Field and see justice was done through the Improvement Commissioners? It was only a few years later that his nephew Joshua was to have his unfortunate experience of Syke's Grammar School.

The oldest brother, William, born in 1786, left Scarborough and became a corn miller in Gateshead and later in Leeds. He married Rachel Watson and they had eight children, one of whom was another John, born in Jarrow in 1821, who came back to Scarborough to be apprenticed to his uncle's grocery business at the top of Bland's Cliff. He worked for three years in his Uncle Joseph's shop on the Pavement in York but following the sudden death of John, he took over the Scarborough shop for his Aunt Jane.

The Scarborough Board of Guardians accepted Rowntree's tender to provision the Workhouse, the prices agreed were:

'black tea 3s. 4d., coffee 10d., pepper 1s. 2d., rice 14s. per cwt., peas 5s. per bushel; sugar 3½d. per lb., salt, 2s. 4d. per cwt.; dip candles 4s. 4d. and rush lights 5s. 4d. per dozen pounds.'

John married Ann Webster in 1853 and they had seven children; their eldest was John Watson Rowntree, born in 1854. This John was educated at Bootham School and became a proprietor of both the grocery business and the café. He joined the School Board on 1883 and later transferred to the Education Committee. He became Mayor of Scarborough in 1906.

Another branch of the family also moved to Scarborough. John's brother, Joseph, born in 1774 at Risborough, took on Low Mill in Pickering; his son, William, born in 1806, started Rowntree's Draper's Store in 1827. His original shop was at 41, 42, 43 Newborough Street but later they moved to Westborough.

Rowntrees' Store, Westborough

William's son, William Stickney Rowntree, born in 1849, was educated at Bootham and University College, London. He continued running the store and also took up the education baton by joining the Scarborough School Board, retiring as Chairman in 1883. He was on the Education Committee together with John Watson Rowntree from the start and became Mayor of Scarborough from 1910 to 1911. His brother, James Henry, also joined the family firm.

St Martin's Grammar School

Forster's Education Act of 1870 that introduced Board Schools may have contributed to the closure of John Swalwell's school thus bringing to an end any control St Mary's Church had of the Grammar School. Mary Craven, the great benefactor of the new Pre-Raphaelite South Cliff Church, St Martin-on-the-Hill, donated £1,000 towards establishing St Martin's Grammar School at 60 Ramshill Road. It remained as such from 1872 to 1922.

Mary Craven was born in Hull in 1819, she lived in Albion Street with her three sisters. Their father was a wealthy doctor in that town, as was the church architect, George Frederick Bodley's father. On their father's retirement, the Craven family came to live in the fashionable part of Scarborough at 5 Esplanade but sadly he died in 1859 and Mary looked upon her contributions to the church as his memorial. She seems to have been quite a character; she selected the first Vicar, the Revd Robert Henning Parr, had her own named seat in the church and is reputed to have been reprimanded for 'purloining flowers from the Spaw'.

St Martin's Grammar School had four headmasters in its 50 year history. The first two, John Wilkes and Arthur Whiteley were clergymen but in 1885, one Thomas Raven took over with a firm hand and no qualifications, earning the school the nickname 'Smartin's'.

The annual charge for a boarder was 40 guineas (a guinea being £1.05); laundry cost 3 guineas a year. Instruction was divided into two sections, the Classical Department charged 10 to 12 guineas annually and the Modern Department only 6 to 8 guineas. Together with two more teachers they covered a curriculum that included English, Latin, French, Mathematics and Science, an extra charge of four and a half guineas was made for German and 15 shillings for games and drill. The Vicar gave a 20 minute session in religious instruction once a week, this was free.

In 1890 there were 50 boys from the age of 12, attending the school; they usually left at 15, having taken public examinations, to work in clerical jobs or the merchant navy. The last headmaster was a Classics graduate from Durham University, Charles Frederick Turnbull. He improved the school in many ways, forming a preparatory school in Albion Road, increasing the staff to seven and adding a fully equipped science laboratory in the old school.

St Martin's Grammar School on Ramshill

The New Grammar Schools

By 1921 however, the North Riding Education Authority had taken control of secondary education. The Municipal

School, an excellent, purpose-built, higher grade school with well-qualified staff and affectionately known as 'The Muni', had been established in Westwood in 1900, catering for both boys and girls at a fee of 2d per week. However, St Martin's Grammar School building was deemed no longer fit for purpose so it was decided to transfer the boys and their headmaster to the Westwood site. The resulting Scarborough Boys' High School had a record that compared well with the best in the country under distinguished headmasters Mr Mayor (1923-6), Raymond King (1926-30) and Henry Marsden (1930-61).

To make room for the St Martin's boys, the girls were removed from the Muni into premises vacated by a private boarding school for girls. Westlands in Westbourne Grove had suffered damage in the Bombardment of Scarborough on 16 December 1914. The girls had left their dormitories to go to breakfast so there had been no casualties; later they marched in orderly style to Seamer Station, caught their trains and went home. The school moved to Eshton Hall near Skipton for the duration of the war.

For the first time, we have girls included in the grammar school system in Scarborough, separate from the boys and in much inferior premises but with a pioneering headmistress, Miss E Glauert, graduate in mathematics of Girton College Cambridge. She moved with her pupils to the new, purpose built school in Sandybed Lane in September 1939, retiring in 1946, after the end of the Second World War. Miss Millicent Woods, also a graduate in mathematics, took over. The third and final headmistress, another highly qualified spinster, graduate in English at Manchester University, was Miss Hilda Briggs who saw the school through to the advent of comprehensive education.

The 1944 Education Act had brought in free secondary education for all pupils, prior to this, fees were charged after the age of 14, unless the pupil had won a free scholarship; the annual fee in Scarborough was £10. In 1959 the boys' grammar school moved premises, this time out of town to

Woodlands Drive. Alec Gardener was the last Headmaster of the boys' grammar school as the North Yorkshire Education Authority decided to make all Scarborough secondary schools comprehensive and mixed; in 1973 it became The Graham School.

And what happened to the Grammar School Trust? A scheme was drawn up by the Charity Commission in 1888 for the formation of the Scarborough United Scholarships Foundation which gathered together *'the foundation known as the Grammar School in the borough of Scarborough'* together with *'the Foundation known as the Falsgrave Trust in the above named borough'*.

Now we need to find out about the Falsgrave Town Trust.

*

PART TWO
Falsgrave Town Trust

Tostig's Legacy

From the Domesday Book we learn that in 1066 Falsgrave, or Wallsgrave as it was written, came under the rule of Tostig, Earl of Northumbria, and comprised 20 villagers, 14 smallholders and seven freemen. Its value that year was £56 but by the time William the Conqueror had ravaged the North of England, it was only worth £1.50 in 1086. There is no entry in this historical document for its larger neighbour because Scarborough did not exist at that time. The Manor of Falsgrave, comprising 10 carucates of land, extended from Staintondale in the north to Filey in the south and inland to Ruston. It also included the villages of Hackness, Burniston, Suffield and Everley. A carucate was the amount of land a team of oxen could plough in a year and a day, taken as 120 acres, and was used for tax purposes.

The small community nestling under the sea-cliff, reputedly founded by Skarthi in 966, had been razed to the ground by Harald Hardrada, King of Norway in 1066. The event is described in Snorri Sturleson's Icelandic saga. Harald's fleet on its journey from Orkney, then under Norwegian rule, was becalmed in Scarborough bay. Harald had climbed the hill, lit a huge bonfire and, using pitchforks, his men had hurled burning timbers onto the houses below where one by one they caught fire. It is hardly surprising that the few survivors swore allegiance to King Harald. The Viking king then proceeded to the Humber with his troops in 300 dragon-headed long ships.

Tostig's father, Godwine Earl of Wessex, was a powerful man; he was married to Gytha and had many children. His daughter Edith married King Edward; of his two sons Harold and Tostig, the first became king of England and the second became Earl of Northumberland. Snorri Sturleson's Icelandic saga mentions a daughter called Velgerde who lived in Scarborough and was married to a Viking, Aki the Tall. While other stories of this time focus on the sighting of Haley's Comet in 1066, the Icelandic saga has Harald Hardrada seeing a troll-wife riding a wolf across the sky when they landed at Scarborough. It goes on to describe both the Battle of Fulford where Aki, who was fighting on the side of the English, was killed, and the ensuing Battle of Stamford Bridge.

The Icelandic sagas were written in the 13th and 14th centuries and are unique

From another translation of Icelandic sagas by Anthony Faulkes, we have the 'Story of Heming' which includes an account of King Edward the Confessor making an earlier visit to Scarborough to feast with Earl Godwine. Tostig tried to trick King Edward into giving him his iron-headed spear by removing the head from his own spear and fashioning a point in the wooden shaft. Edward saw him for the coveting person he was and took his brother Harold back to live with him. A man by the name of Leif was living at Harold's court, he was the skilled Heming in disguise, hero of the saga; it was he who taught Harold all the skills of warfare. Historically Heming was the brother of the Viking chieftain Thorkell who ravaged England on behalf of King Svein Forkbeard of Denmark, father of King Cnut (Canute).

Why should the Norwegian king have been sailing past Scarborough in the first place? 1066 was a year of three crowned kings of England. King Edward the Confessor died on 5 January leaving no family; the contenders to the throne were 15 year old Edgar the Aethling; Harold Godwinson from Wessex, brother of Edward's wife; Harald Hardrada, King of Norway, and William Duke of Normandy, his first cousin once removed. Harold Godwinson was first to the mark; before anyone could stop him, he had himself crowned king on 6 January.

Brothers Harold and Tostig Godwinson were deadly enemies. Tostig, who was married to Judith of Flanders, a cousin of William, Duke of Normandy, had already been exiled by King Edward at Harold's instigation. Judith was a very pious lady who endowed Durham Cathedral and had illuminated manuscripts made. In 1055, King Edward had instated Tostig as Earl of Northumbria, which covered virtually the whole country north of the Humber. However, as Tostig could not keep control of the region and possibly because he was too friendly with King Malcolm III of Scotland for Edward's liking, he was replaced by Morcar, younger brother of Edwin Earl of Mercia, in 1065.

This resulted in Tostig deciding to wage war against his brother. To begin with he tried to get William on side, without success, but Harald Hardrada, King of Norway, was willing to help and the two had joined forces at the River Tyne before sailing down the coast and calling in at Scarborough. The first battle took place on 20 September outside York at Fulford Gate. Harald and Tostig's long ships, laden with troops and supplies, had made their way via the Humber up the River Ouse to Riccall, where they made camp. The young, inexperienced earls, Morca and Edwin, unaware that their ally, King Harold, was on his way north, left the safety of the city walls. They were badly defeated, thousands died on both sides in the Battle of Fulford.

Five days later and some ten miles away, the second battle took place at Stamford Bridge, this time Harald Hardrada and Tostig fought King Harold. Victory came to King Harold, who had marched his troops from the south coast where he was anticipating William's invasion. Both Tostig and Harald Hardrada were killed; it is suggested that Harold cut off Tostig's head and that Harald, King of Norway, died with an arrow in his throat. From the 300 ships that brought the troops, only 24 were needed to make the return voyage to Norway so great was the carnage. Tostig was eventually buried in York Minster. Judith, his widow, went to Denmark with their three young children; she later married the Duke of Bavaria.

Meanwhile William Duke of Normandy and his men had reached Pevensey Bay on 28 September. King Harold marched his troops back the length of the country to Hastings and the third and final battle for the kingship of England was fought on 14 October. Although the two armies were well matched, the English broke ranks when the Normans feigned retreat. Tradition has it that Harold was killed by an arrow piercing his eye, though this is disputed. On the death of their king, the English soldiers fled, leaving William as conqueror. Although Edgar the Aethling was appointed by the Witan as uncrowned king, William was crowned on Christmas Day 1066 in Westminster Abbey.

We have an alternative version of events in the 'Story of Heming': a woman looking for survivors after the battle, found King Harold badly wounded but still alive. After she had nursed him back to health, he went to live in a hermit's cell in Canterbury, waited on by Heming. When he eventually died, King William gave him a royal funeral; Heming then lived to old age in the same cell.

William the Conqueror carved up the country, rewarding his family and favourites with land. It wasn't until around 1130 that his great-nephew William le Gros, Lord of Holderness, Count of Aumerle (Albermarle) chose to build a castle, probably of wood, on Scarborough's headland. This was the reason for the development of the town which then overtook Falsgrave in importance. Stone from the Falsgrave quarry, which was probably on the slopes of Jacob's Mount, was used in the later building of the castle.

The Franciscan Friars

The town of Scarborough relied on the springs in Falsgrave for its water supply, thanks originally to the ingenuity of the Franciscan monks, the Grey Friars, who arrived in Scarborough and settled in what is now St Sepulchre Street around 1239. We learn from Bulmer's transcriptions from the early 1820s that the area around Falsgrave was *'disafforested and annexed to the liberties of Scarborough in the 40th year of Henry III'* (around 1256). Henry III ordered the Sheriff of Yorkshire to provide food for them one day every week. When they fell foul of the Cistercian monks in St Mary's Church they moved out of town.

On 11 August 1245, the King gave them a licence to build a convent on land *'lying between Cukewaldhull and the watercourse called Milnebec'*, land donated by William son of Robert de Morpath, the village was known as

Hatterbord. Milnebec is the stream that still flows along Lady Edith's Drive from Throxenby Mere, under Scalby Road, down Woodlands Ravine, through the Glen into Peasholm Lake before joining the sea. Jack Binns tells us that the Scarborough Archaeological Society excavated the site shortly before the Technical College was built on Scalby Road. Among the remains of houses they found one dating from around 1245 that had been re-built in stone, this could have belonged to the Franciscans.

In 1283 the burgesses granted Robert of Scarborough, Dean of York, a spring on Falsgrave Moor at 'Guildhuscliff' to make a conduit to benefit the Franciscans. Fortunately Robert, who was a member of the influential Ughtred family of Scagglethorpe, left 100 marks in his will to provide for this as he died before it was finished. According to Thomas Hinderwell, the Knights Hospitaller of St John of Jerusalem gave a commission to dedicate their church to the Holy Sepulchre on 20 March 1306 and later on 27 July a commission to dedicate its altars. This church disappeared in the Reformation but Jack Binns suggests that the Buttercross, which originally stood in the Market Place, not far from St Sepulchre Street, could have been part of a pinnacle from the Holy Sepulchre Church. The site was later used by the Methodists to build their church.

It was not until 1319 that a licence was granted for the stone-lined, lead watercourse which ran underground and freely supplied all Scarborough people no matter what their status, with a good supply of Falsgrave water for the next 500 years. The water was stored in three stone troughs, the Upper Conduit on the corner of Newborough and St Thomas Street, then the Middle Conduit at the top of St Sepulchre Street. The Lower Conduit was below the market in what is now Princess Street, it had a pump and a pub nearby called 'The Old Brass Tap'. Eventually the Bailiffs were given responsibility for the upkeep of the water supply.

Tom Bennett's picture of the Old Brass Tap in Old Conduit Street

Falsgrave had its own place of worship, in 1428 St Clement's Chapel was answerable to St Mary's Church. A bequest was made to its fabric in 1496 and the last that was heard of it was in 1566 when Queen Elizabeth granted possession of it to Thomas Blackway and Francis Barker. It probably stood near the Guildhouse at the head of Ramsdale. Ramsdale was so named after the wild garlic that grew there, a plant that is often associated with the presence of monks in earlier times; it gave its name to the stream that ran from Falsgrave, down the Valley and into the sea. Excavating a site in Falsgrave Park, the Scarborough Archaeological Society discovered where the Franciscans had tapped the springs; a stone building was erected by the residents of Falsgrave in 18th century on the site of the original 1319 Franciscan conduit house. On the 1782 map of Falsgrave the site is named as 'Conduit House Allotment'.

Falsgrave Endowed School

Falsgrave continued as a township separate from Scarborough until it was officially united in 1890. By 1835 the Boundary Commissioners had decided that *'Falsgrave already forms part of the Borough'* but, they recommended that the village be kept as such. There was already a school that had been built by subscription, the decision to build having been made on 3 February 1806 at a meeting convened by the Constables of Falsgrave.

Two of the ten constables elected each year for one year in Scarborough were for Falsgrave. This unpaid role required them to try to keep the peace in their spare time, the hue and cry would also be led by them. They were also responsible for controlling the vermin in this rural village as an entry in their records on 31 March 1809 shows:

'whereas the number of sparrows in this Township has become so great as to be a public grievance from the injury they do amongst corn, and by way of encouragement to boys for checking the breed of such noxious vermin, it is resolved this day, at a meeting

convened by proper notice for sundry business relative to the Town, that the Overseers of the Poor shall give three pence a dozen for all the sparrows killed and brought to them, and one penny a dozen for the sparrows' eggs, and to charge such outlay in their accounts accordingly.'

The Constables had to account for their income, in February 1710 they recorded the letting of a small field for £2.12s.0d. An Act of Parliament (15 George 3) on property in 1775 is often referred to in the documents and we are given the names of the fields that were in their charge until 1888 namely Quarry Bank, Bell Corner, Clay Piece and Oxcliff. In addition we have Fountain's Field with mention of a sum, not exceeding £1 per acre per annum allowed to its tenant, *'in order that a bull should be kept by him for use of the resident inhabitants of Falsgrave'.*

Falsgrave Endowed School

Further to building the school, the meeting on 3 February 1806 decided to include a house for a poor person on Parish Relief and cater for six free scholars alongside the paying pupils. The first of these to be selected were John Cowthorpe, Christopher Tate, Robert Walker, Francis Anderson, Grace Dawson and Elizabeth Tate. Schoolmasters were to be chosen by giving their names to the Constables, they would then be elected by the inhabitants at a convened meeting, one vote each per resident freeholder *'whether his property be house or land'*. In order to attract a good teacher, they resolved that:

> *'the Constables for the time being, do yearly, and every year for ever pay out of the rents of the Town Lands five guineas to the School Master.'*

Mr Richard Harland was duly elected to start that very day and the schoolroom was to be housed in a tenement until the school was built. The six children

> *'of indigent parents residing in this Town shall be annually elected'*

and would be paid for at the rate of 12 shillings per year, each. It was stipulated that they should:

> *'be instructed as carefully as any other children there, and be furnished with suitable books at <u>the expense of the Constables</u>.'*

The money to pay for the building of Falsgrave Endowed School was raised by public subscription. We have a full list of the subscribers and the suppliers of materials for the building of the school, as produced for the Town Meeting the following year, some people appear on both lists. The Overseers paid £3 and amongst the others, there were four donations of 10 guineas each, thirteen of one guinea and five of half a guinea. Amongst the contributors listed are two farmers, a publican, a tanner, a brick and stone merchant, a timber merchant and a joiner. The bell, for which Richard Sawdon paid £6 15s to Percy and Thomas, was an important item, it had to be rung every day but Sunday at 8.00am and 1.00pm thus providing a useful service to the whole community. For his guinea subscription, Robert Coates did quite well as he supplied 8,700 bricks, 1,000 tiles, did the walling, tiling and plastering, claimed for sundry cartage, completed the stone for subscribers names and the sundial and received 4s 6d drink money for the workers, resulting in business worth a total of £52 14s 4d. There was a shortfall of 13s. 2d. when the final balance sheet was drawn up.

Mr Harland, the Master, was discharged in 1809, no reason given, to be replaced by Robert Hopper. Andrew Brown stayed for one year from 1814 to 1815 then Thomas Webster took over until 1823. Francis Etty was teaching there in 1834, then George Beech stayed until 1841; Richard Tindale took over until 1847 when John Paylor arrived, by which time the annual salary had risen to £15. The children had to pay 1d a week for reading or 2d for reading, writing and arithmetic. It would appear the number of paying pupils varied but in 1849 the public meeting agreed to form two classes for the 18 pupils, divided not by age or ability but with nine elected *'from middle families with large families'* and the other nine *'from Labouring Poor'*.

The various Education Acts and an increase in population impacted on Falsgrave. The Infant Department was opened in March 1873 for 128 pupils and the Girls' Department for 180 was added later. The boys were accommodated at that time in All Saints Church of England Boys' School but in June 1884 Falsgrave Board School opened its Boys' Department to accommodate 206 pupils. We learn that in 1890 Mr J H Yewdall was its headmaster, Miss A Carr the head mistress and Miss H Oates the Infants' mistress, by which time free, compulsory education was available to all up to the age of 10 and to 13 for some. The old school was redundant.

The Township of Falsgrave

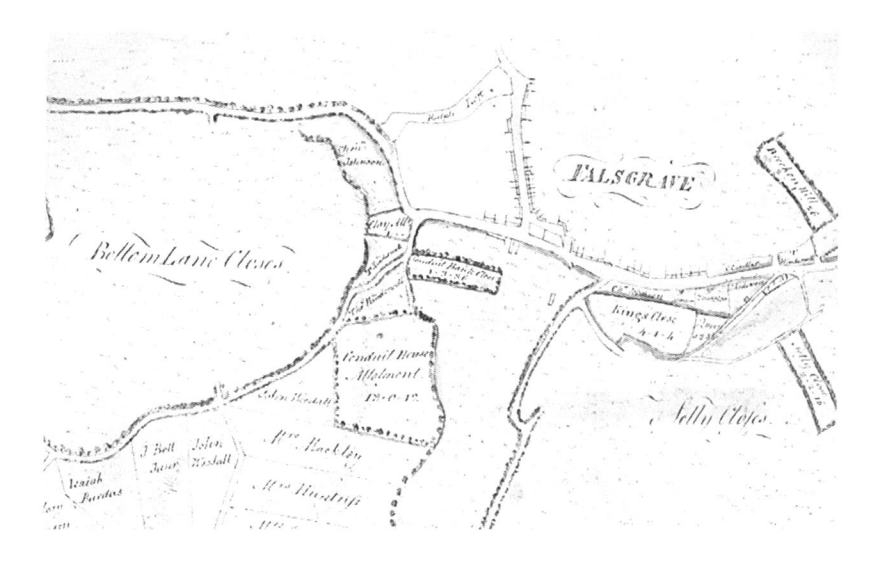

Map of Falsgrave. 18th Century

Perhaps we should wander round village of Falsgrave as it would have been in the early 19th century with its school standing proudly near the Wesleyan Chapel on Bakehouse Hill. Between these two buildings was an arched portico leading to the Strawberry Gardens, a place to stroll in the summer. Pigot's Directory of 1828 tells us that the pleasure garden was much frequented by visitors and inhabitants alike. It was established under the auspices of the Duchess of Leeds, wife of George William Frederick Osborne, 6th Duke of Leeds, Lord Lieutenant of the North Riding. Cole's 'Scarborough Guide of 1825' attributes ownership of the Subscription Gardens to Mr Pearson. For 2s 6d for one person or 5s for a family for the season, visitors could gather and eat fruit, strawberries, gooseberries etc., the charge for a single visit was one shilling. You could sit in any of the numerous summerhouses to drink tea and take in the beautiful views of Scarborough Castle, the North Sands and

Oliver's Mount. In the 1835 Directory we find Richard Pearson was also selling beer. The arches to these gardens have since been moved to The Crescent and stand in the garden at Londesborough Lodge.

In addition to Falsgrave's houses, farms and cottages for farm workers there were shops, public houses and a variety of rural industries. Mr. George Cooke had a very considerable tannery near the corner of North Street and Town Street (Scalby Road and Stepney Road), William Goodwill was a shoemaker in North Street and there was also a stonemason's yard belonging to George Coates. A timber yard stood on the back lane, Mile End Place (Cambridge Place) it belonged to Robert Jackson who was also a wheelwright. William Linskill was a Grocer and Flour Dealer and James Wood offered Hair Cutting and Perfumeries.

The township had a pinfold near here, a structure for holding animals, often stray ones, until their owner collected them. There were cow houses and a stone-built dairy farm on the far side of Town Street that in 1881 belonged to the Stephenson family. Their daughter, Emma, married Albert Morley, whose son Clifford was secretary to the SUSF. There was also a printing works and a pottery industry; bricks and tiles were made possibly at a site off the Seamer Road near Barry's Lane and as late as WW2, Malton's Brickworks in what is now Malvern Crescent, housed a rifle range.

Thomas Robinson was given permission from the Bailiffs to build a new windmill in 1784 in the area known as Bracken Hill. Its sails were damaged in a storm in 1898 but it still stands, renovated as a hotel in Mill Street, off Victoria Road. We see from directories of the 1800s that Falsgrave had its share of public houses too. Thomas Robinson's 'Elephant' was taken over by Christopher Bourdas by 1840, Joseph Carlisle ran the 'New Inn' and Thomas Craine had 'The Waggon and Horses'. Francis Morris' 'White Horse' changed colour by 1840 to become

'The Grey Horse'. Mr Morris is also listed as a blacksmith, professions that often ran together.

Publicans' licences were granted by the corporation and there was much suspicion concerning the rigging of votes at election time. The Scarborough Corporation was brought to trial in November 1833, the ensuing report by Dwarris and Rumball, two of His Majesty's Commissioners was very damning about the state of the corporation. Local men, Samuel Byron, a magistrate who lived in West Ayton; John Hesp, solicitor; George Davies, described as a gentleman living in Sidney Place and solicitor William Page of Newborough, cross-examined the committee of local worthies. They were John W Woodall, Town Clerk; John Woodall, Bailiff; William Thornton, Bailiff; Edward Hebden, Coroner; Henry Fowler, Coroner; Anthony Beswick; William Travis and the Corporation's Solicitor, Edward Donner.

Among the many charges was the expenditure of £37 during the election the previous year. William Travis' answer that it had been distributed amongst the poor, made Samuel Byron explode with anger – he said 2 guineas each had been given to 18 publicans and that the licence had recently been granted to Bleach House because it belonged to a member of the Corporation. Henry Fowler, possibly defending himself, said it had been granted 'for the public good' because it was on the road to the Mere. The outcome can have made little difference to its Publican, Samuel Taylor from Stainsacre near Whitby, on the 1861 Census he was still the innkeeper at the age of 71.

Bleach House, also known as the Crown Tavern, stood where the present day Valley Road joins Westbourne Grove; the building would originally have been used for washing and bleaching the sails for fishing boats. York Road came from Scarborough through Ramsdale Valley, past the Mere and continued to Seamer; the stretch leading from Seamer Road to the South Cliff was known as Bleach House Lane or Washbeck.

The 'Royal Mail' coach would use this route into Scarborough, it left the Black Swan in York at seven each morning arriving at the Bell Inn on Bland's Cliff; it made the return journey to York at three in the afternoon. There were regular coaches to all parts of the country, 'The Old True Blue' travelled to and from Leeds (Sunday excepted) 'The Prince Blucher' similarly, leaving from The Talbot at seven in the morning; all these coaches passed through Ayton, Snainton, Yeddingham and Malton. The 'Wellington' and the 'Magna Carta' travelled to Hull via Bridlington Quay, Driffield and Beverley. The London coach, the 'Express' took a similar route, it left alternately from the Talbot and the New Inn at six in the morning, stopping at Barton, Lincoln and Peterborough. An alternative means of travelling to London was by sea in the 'The Oak', 'The Aid' or 'The Endeavour'.

For those wishing to travel north to Stockton, the 'Union' left alternately from the Bell or the Talbot Inn every afternoon at half past four, it travelled through Whitby and Guisborough. You could also make arrangements to get to Guisborough or Stockton with George Frank from the White Bear or William Cooper from the Elephant and Castle every Thursday and Saturday.

The arrival of the railway brought the demise of the stage coach. Washbeck gave its name to the viaduct that carried the railway line over the valley. We find the excursion platform that catered for the new class of day-trippers, mainly from industrial West Riding, was called Washbeck Station. The railway had a great effect on the township of Falsgrave, just as the gentry had houses built on the South Cliff, so houses were built in this area for the workers, completely changing its nature and ambiance.

St James' Church was opened in 1885 as a mission chapel to cater for the growth in population. The road from Scarborough, Falsgrave Walk, was developed, some of the gentry, including ship owners, had houses built in Hinderwell Place, Belgravia (now Belgrave Square), Victoria

Place and Grove Terrace thus merging Scarborough with what had been a separate rural community. The Falsgrave Endowed School ceased to function on 25 September 1884 although the cash book continues until September 1888 showing a balance in hand of £253.12s. 3d. One pivotal gentleman in the amalgamation of the Grammar School Trust and the Falsgrave Town Trust in 1888 was William Ascough, Secretary to the Board of Education, who came to live at 13 West Grove Terrace, Falsgrave in 1879 - more of him later.

Resistance to Change

The Falsgrave Town Trust was considering joining with the Grammar School Trust to form Scarborough United Scholarships Foundation. They held a meeting on 21 July 1886 to discuss the final arrangements for the setting up of the SUSF. All was not plain sailing; Mr Wrightson in particular held strong views against relinquishing the Trust and voiced them at this well attended gathering. Many people said they had not had a chance to read the details even though many meetings had already been held; some said they did not understand what it was about. There was a discussion around being allowed to remove the stone from Quarry Bank although it was suggested that none had been removed in the past forty years.

The newspaper records this as *'a long desultory discussion'* but eventually the motion to accept the proposal was agreed when Councillor W S Rowntree assured everyone that the rights of the Falsgrave people were included in the plan. In the final wording of the Scheme presented on 17 May 1888 we read:

> *'in the matter of the Foundation known as the Falsgrave Town Trust ...*
> *(1) So long as the conduit or pump known as the Falsgrave Village Pump is used for the common supply*

of water for the inhabitants of Falsgrave a sum not exceeding £3 16s 6d may be required to defray expenses of repairs

(2) ... a sum not exceeding £1 reduction in rent to the tenant to keep a Bull for use by the inhabitants of Falsgrave.'

The Governing Body had to include three members elected by the Freeholders of the township of Falsgrave. The first of these were John Featherstone, Farmer, of Scalby Road; James Bland, Builder of Gladstone Street and George Pullon, Ironmonger, who became the Secretary and was then living at 12 West Grove Terrace, one time neighbour to William Ascough.

Included in the assets acquired by SUSF were the school building and the fields, Bell Corner, Quarry Bank, Fountain's Field, Oxcliffe and Claypiece. Hidden away in the depths of the Library are the legal documents giving details of their sale. The first to be sold was:

'a school house or building lately used and known as the Falsgrave Parish School with buildings and yard on Bakehouse Hill, Falsgrave'

Permission to sell was given by Daniel Robert Fearon, Secretary to the Board of Charity Commissioners on 9 August 1889.

Ten years later on 4 December Valentine Fowler held an auction in the George Hotel for the sale of Fountains Fields. They comprised a total of six acres, three hundred square yards with frontages to Stepney and Scalby Roads and were bounded by lands belonging to William Malton on the north-west and John Woodall Woodall on the south-east. H E Donner was the solicitor.

The sale of Oxcliffe and Claypiece on 4 November 1901 was conducted by the solicitors Watts, Kitching and Donner. Frank Horner, manufacturer of bricks and tiles, who was living in Alexandra Park, said he had known both pieces of land. Oxcliffe was near Stepney on the High Road from Scarborough to Ayton, it comprised 9 acres, 1 ro0d, 20 perches and was bounded on the north by land belonging to G S Nesfield and to the west by land belonging to Lord Londesborough. Claypiece, on Spring Hill, at the junction of the Falsgrave and Stepney Roads, was also bounded by land belonging to G S Nesfield. Unsurprisingly it was sold to George Smart Nesfield, who was a Brewer, and his sister Emily Nesfield.

Valentine Fowler sold Bell Corner and Quarry Bank by auction at his Huntriss Row Auction Room in May 1902. They were purchased by Ellen Malton, widow, for £3,200. While searching for Bell Corner I discovered Bell Mansion in Long Room Street (now known as the Georgian House in St Nicholas Street). Mr Bell, a respectable confectioner from York at a time when his art was greatly prized by the gentry, used to spend the season here with his family. In 1804, one of his daughters fell in love with a young officer of the militia, stationed at the castle but Father did not approve. She was found strangled and thrown down the cliff near Cayton Bay. Many years later, the officer confessed to her murder although at the time his fellow officers had given him an alibi. There are many stories of people seeing a ghost wearing pink crinoline in the house.

The Bell Corner in question was near the right-angled bend on the east side of Stepney Hill near Jacob's Mount. It comprised *'3 roods, 31½ perches or thereabouts, 306 on the Ordnance Plan'*; at the time it had a shed for a slaughterhouse and was used by J W Drake for cattle and horses. Quarry Bank *'2 acres 1 rood 36 perches, 228 on the Ordnance Plan'* adjoined it, near the footpath by Jacob's Ladder, the continuation of Spring Hill that led to Barron's Farm. This was probably the quarry that had provided the stones for the building of the castle. Apparently Frank A Tugwell, architect, had advised. The sale had been agreed by Revd Richard Frederick Lefevre Blunt; Charles Coleridge

Mackarness; John Stephenson; William Ascough, Clerk; William Sanderson, Schoolmaster; Henry Merry Cross; James Bland, Builder and George Pullon, Ironmonger, all SUSF Trustees.

Thus the ancient legacy of Falsgrave with its historical field names was merged with the Grammar School Trust to form the Scarborough United Scholarships Foundation in order to improve the opportunities of future generations of children. Next we will discover why education was changing.

*

PART THREE
Acts and Influences

A Changing Society

During the 19th Century society throughout the country was changing more rapidly than ever before. Mechanisation was overtaking traditional crafts, particularly in spinning and weaving; traction engines were replacing farm labourers and the development of the railways made it possible for ordinary people to travel around the country. What became known as the industrial revolution was enticing people away from rural areas into the cities where factories, hungry for a growing workforce, devoured the unsuspecting.

Scarborough South Bay around 1850

Changing governments had difficulty deciding what line to take, particularly in the matter of education. There were bitter ideological disputes between the Whigs and the Tories as to whether or not the population should be educated. Many thought that if the lower orders became better educated, they would not want to be fed to menial jobs with the result that factories would no longer make profits for their owners. The counter-argument was for everyone to benefit and have better opportunities. To help us understand why our charities were set up we will look at the way the new laws affected the people of Scarborough.

1835 Municipal Corporations Reform Act

This act had been devised to do away with self-perpetuating burgesses, in Scarborough's case families who had governed the town from the Common Hall on Sandside since the 13th century. Only male ratepayers and male lodgers whose rent was £10 or more, if they had lived in the town for three years or more were given the vote; women were not emancipated until after the First World War.

Scarborough was to have two wards, North and South, with the boundary drawn by two barristers, Fletcher Rainstock and William Gray, appointed by the Lord Chief Justice. Their letter to the Home Secretary, dated 15 October 1835, designated this boundary line: it ran down the centre of the road coming in from Falsgrave, through Newborough Bar, along Newborough Street, Carr Street, Leading Post Street, Church Stair Street, Castle Gate, round the southern boundary of the Castle to the sea.

Each ward would elect nine Councillors to the Borough Council for a period of three years at a time: one third was to be elected annually. From their number the Councillors were to choose the Mayor, who would hold office for one year, and six Aldermen, whose office was for six years. The Town Clerk and Treasurer were paid officers and the accounts were to be properly audited. These new Borough Councils were required to form a Police Force and, only if they so wished, they could take over such social improvements as proper drainage and street cleaning. Scarborough's council took over the water supply little changed since it was inherited from the Cistercian monks.

THE POPULATION OF SCARBOROUGH.

Census, March 31st, 1851.

Scarborough and Falsgrave	Inhabited Houses.	Uninhabited Houses.	Building.	Males.	Females.	Total.
Scarborough—						
North Ward..	1616	136	22	3274	4004	7278
South Ward..	1048	66	1	2065	2744	4809
	2664	202	23	5339	6748	12,087
Falsgrave	176	9	3	328	429	757
Total	2840	211	26	5667	7177	12,844

Whether the act totally achieved its aim could be questioned as some family names that appeared on the old lists of burgesses, like Tindall, Woodall and Fowler, continued as mayors under the new system as late as 1907.

Forster's Education Act

Education had been available to those with privileged backgrounds and to those who managed to avail themselves of benevolent charitable organisations or individuals such as the various denominations of the Church or the new wave of industrialists who provided education for their workers.

In Pigot's Directory of 1834 we find a list of Scarborough's Academies and Schools. There was a proliferation of boarding schools in Queen Street; Miss Addison had one for ladies while Robert Addison had one for gents, both occupying number 32. Jane and Sarah Irvine had another boarding school for ladies at number 27. Further down the street at number 21 we find Margaret King's boarding and day school and William Wood also had a boarding school in Queen Street, no number given. If we cross Newborough Street, where Sarah Bulmer had a day school, we find William Potter's establishment at 5 King Street.

Not far away we have Richard Suggitt in St Helen's Square, Timothy Swift's subscription school for Infants was in St Sepulchre Street: Ainsworth's Scarborough Guide of 1827 suggests that it came under the management of the Lancastrian School and catered for 150 children. In the same street Thomas Peckston had his boarding and day school at number 10. Richard Tindall was in Cross Street; John Willis had a boarding and day school in Auborough Street and Ambrose Tyson a day school in Castle Gate. We pass the Nautical School at 52 Longwestgate run by Robert Middleton Clough and proceed up the hill to the Grammar School with Revd J Skelton in charge. Somewhat away from the rest, George Bullock chose to have his school in Huntriss Row.

The Charity schools at the time were the Amicable Schools in Dewsbery Walk with John Mitchell and Ann Marshall and almost opposite on Castle Road was the Lancastrian School with John Gillott and Sophia Denton. We find the School of Industry on Cook's Row with Mistress Chatwin in charge. Falsgrave has its Endowed School run by Francis Etty and the only other village mentioned is Seamer with Denison's Charity School.

The government woke up to the idea that the work force in other countries where state funded education was provided was more productive than ours so they decided to look into the matter. The Act of 1870, known as Forster's Education Act, made local councils responsible for providing education for children between the ages of 5 and 13 years through local rates. Each Town Council was to set up a School Board of locally elected members and establish Elementary Board Schools. Each pupil paid a fee, usually two pence a week, as free elementary education was not introduced until 1891 and a totally free secondary education had to wait for the ground-breaking 1944 Education Act.

Six years after Forster's Act, compulsory school attendance was recommended in the Factories Act in order to abolish child labour, it was achieved in 1880. Blind and deaf children were included in 1893 and 'defective and epileptic children' in 1899 when the upper age limit was set at 12 years.

The Scarborough School Board

Every householder in the town, male or female, had been allowed to cast 2 votes on an accumulated system in accordance with Forster's Act. John Woodall Woodall, Deputy Returning Officer, declared the results of the first election of the School Board on 4 February 1871 which are recorded in their minute book:

John Buttrick	3058
Richard Frederick Lefevre Blunt	2346
William Foster Rooke	2109
William Rowntree	1992
John Walker	1745
John Tindall	1639
James Acworth	1553
George Porrett	1481
Henry Merry Cross	1371

The unsuccessful candidates were:

Robert Champley	1347
Richard Peacock	1318
Alfred John Tugwell	1020
Nicholas Delamare	129
Charles Thackwray	19

The first meeting was held on Thursday, the 23rd day of February 1871 in the Town Hall. At that time the Town Hall was in Castle Road opposite the junction with North Marine Road, built for the purpose together with a Court House, in 1867. From 1800 when the Council moved up from Sandside, William Newstead's Assembly Rooms at 22 Long Room Street had been hired by the Corporation as the Town Hall. It still had gaming and billiard tables, a ballroom with three beautiful gas chandeliers and an orchestra; it also offered forty well-appointed bedrooms. The Clerk to the Magistrates, victualler Edward Donner, was able to let it out for concerts and public meetings. The Woodall family were the next occupants, eventually they sold it to the Corporation and now the present Town Hall stands on that same site.

The Members of the School Board came from differing backgrounds; Mr John Buttrick was a Primitive Methodist Preacher; Reverend Richard Frederick Lefevre Blunt was the Vicar of St Mary's Church; Dr. William Foster Rooke was a practising physician who was then the Mayor of Scarborough; Reverend John Walker was Canon of St Peter's Roman Catholic Church; Mr. John Tindall, son of Robert Tindall the shipbuilder, was a shipping agent, he later became a private banker. Mr. William Rowntree was a draper, Mr. George Porrett a druggist and Mr. Henry Merry Cross was the Collector of the Poor Rate.

They selected Reverend James Acworth L.L.D., aged 73, as the first Chairman. He had retired to Scarborough in 1863 having been President of the Northern Baptist Society from 1836 to 1863 at their academy, Horton College, which he had had relocated to Rawdon. His undoubted credentials also included the office of President of the Mechanics Institute in the Bradford area. His Scarborough address was 3 Rawdon Villas, Ramshill Road where he lived next door to Joshua Rowntree (MP 1886 – 1892). John Tindall was the Vice Chairman and Mr George Dippie was appointed Clerk to the Board on 13 March with a salary of £60 per calendar year.

The role of the School Board was to ensure there were school places for all children between the ages of 5 and 13, at 2d a week in school fees. The Board was controlled by the Secretary for the Education Department through the Registrar General. With guidance from Revd E W Crabtree HMI, who attended the School Board Meeting on 5 October 1871, they divided the town into six districts and organised a census of eligible children, paying the enumerators one penny per house returned. From this they decided which areas of the town needed schools and arranged the finances through the Public Works Loan Commission.

Competitions were arranged to choose the architects' designs; appropriate sites for the schools were purchased; building firms were selected; advertisements for teachers were placed in 'The Schoolmaster' and 'The Christian World'. The School Board also determined the teachers' salaries and what they should teach. School hours were fixed from 9 am to noon and 1.30 pm to 4 pm; at the opening and closing of the school day the children were to say 'The Lord's Prayer' and a responsible teacher was to read from the Bible and give instruction but no attempt had to be made to attach children to any particular denomination. The dates of all holidays were decided by the Board: on one occasion they gave a day's holiday for the visit of the Channel Fleet.

The site selected for the Central Board Schools was in Trafalgar Street West; Longwestgate School developed in *'the property known as the White House'* formerly the home of Robert Tindall, and Falsgrave Infants' School was to be built in Town Street, Falsgrave. They were all duly opened in 1874. The running of the Lancasterian School was transferred to the School Board the same year.

Lancasterian schools were based on Quaker Joseph Lancaster's model under the 'monitorial system' whereby monitors taught groups, mainly by rote, under the guidance of one teacher. These schools had been set up all around the country, their aim was to educate the poor whilst keeping down the costs. Scarborough's school had been opened in 1827 in Castle Road but transferred to new premises in St Mary's Walk in 1861; Joshua Rowntree was its Secretary and Lord Derwent was Chairman of the Trustees.

Since Pigot's Directory of 1834, we now have St Thomas' National School on East Sandgate; All Saints National School situated between Falsgrave and Londesborough Road (it had to be rebuilt after a fire in 1879) and St Peter's Roman Catholic School in Auborough Street.

The attendance figures for *'all efficient elementary schools, including Board Schools'* were provided by the schools at a meeting on 10 November 1874. They show the number of children on the registers in Scarborough totalled 3,515: the figures for average attendance were 2,299 while those pupils actually present totalled 2,814. This demonstrates that truancy was a problem especially when the children were needed to contribute to the family income during the busy season or with the fishing.

In August 1873 Thomas Aspin and William Kennedy had been appointed as Attendance Officers. Kennedy resigned his post in October 1882; he had been convicted of indecently assaulting his niece whom he had rescued from an Army Orphan School in London. Many School Board meetings were taken up with reports from the Attendance Officers, sometimes the justices and the Constable had to be involved and occasionally the miscreants would be sent to the Industrial School in Hull.

Mr John Brown was appointed Head Master of Central Boys' School on an annual salary of £150; his wife as Mistress of Central Girls' School had a lesser salary of £90. Mr Foord Potter was paid £60 as assistant master in the boys' school while Miss Rodgers' salary as assistant mistress was £40. Miss Esther Fowler, who had come from Sussex, was paid a salary of £90 as Mistress of the Infants' School and Miss Darnell, assistant mistress in the Infants' School received £40. Pupil teachers were paid £8 in their first year, £10 in their second year, £12 in their third year, £16 in their fourth year and £20 in their fifth year.

In 1878, George Dippie was appointed to the more lucrative position of Town Clerk leaving vacant the job of Clerk to the School Board. Of the 114 applicants for the post, Mr Ascough was the only one called for interview. He was offered the post with a salary of £175 for twelve calendar months. Did they realise, I wonder, what a momentous decision they had made and what a far-reaching effect this gentleman would have on the education and well-being of the children of Scarborough?

William Ascough in Burnley

William's remarkable climb in Victorian times from son of a mill worker to clerk to a School Board is worth looking into and may hold the clue to this gentleman's lifelong dedication to the education of children, particularly to those from poorer families.

We leave behind Scarborough's fresh clean air and beautiful coastal scenery to travel to the smoke laden mill town of Burnley where William was born in 1849. His parents, William and Hannah Ascough, had moved with their five children from rural Hunton near Bedale in Yorkshire's North Riding around 1837. They found employment in the Lancashire cotton mills. Their crowded back-to-back house at 5 Clarke Street was close to Parson's Cotton Mill, where father William worked in the warehouse and four of their children eventually joined him as power loom weavers, possibly from the age of nine. One brother, Wilson, became a blacksmith and later moved to Kilton in Cleveland to work in the iron mines, Anna, his sister joined him and married a pedlar in Brotton so we may gather that a good education was not available to the older siblings.

Parsons Mill was owned by John Moore and his son Henry. In the 1851 census John describes himself as a Master Spinner and Manufacturer employing 229 men, 178 women, 79 boys and 85 girls. He was hard hit by the Cotton Famine but 20 years later his son's entry on the 1871 census gives the total number of employees in the mill, men women and children, as 571. Children were sent into the mills to work because their families could not afford to do otherwise. Robert Baker, a Factory Inspector in Oldham in 1862, recorded that boy and girl "helpers" were paid 5s 6d per week of which 3d was deducted for school fees. Groceries cost 5d per pound for beef (not best quality), 2s 6d a pound for tea, 8lbs rice cost one shilling whilst a 4lb loaf of bread cost five pence, rent for the house would have been between 2s 8d and 4s a week.

Hannah Ascough had a large, hungry family to feed on a limited income, this would have been made even more difficult when work was short due to the American Civil War and the supply of raw cotton from the southern states was blocked. William, the ninth of nine children according to the 1851 census, attended St James' Church of England School where, at the age of fourteen, he became a pupil teacher. Burnley also boasted a thriving Mechanics Institute and a Church Literary Institute. Whist attending school, William was also an active member of the Burnley Athenian Club Literary Society. An article in the Burnley Advertiser of 13 January 1866 reported that W Ascough's recitation 'Mary Queen of Scots' was much admired, in April he was awarded a prize for his essay on 'Self Culture'.

The Burnley Gazette recorded on 25 January 1868:

'Many of our readers will be glad to learn that Mr William Ascough of St James' School, and Mr Horatio Harrison have been successful in the competition for scholarships at the Durham Training College for schoolmasters.'

So William spent the next two years studying in Durham where he qualified for his Schoolmaster's Certificate. On his application form William gave St James' School as his address so it is possible that the school, under the guidance of the Vicar, Revd Hugh Stamer, had set up boarding facilities for 'pauper' pupils during these hard times.

Relief Committees were set up in all the Lancashire mill towns to alleviate the deprivation. Burnley was no exception; of their twelve thousand millworkers, nine thousand were out of work by the end of 1862. The Burnley Advertiser of 15 November that year reported on the Committee's weekly meeting. Among its 27 members we find the newly appointed Mayor, John Moore Esq. of Palace House, took the Chair. There were two councillors, 16 clergymen, including Revd H Stamer and Revd A T Parker, seven other gentlemen and Sir JPK Shuttleworth.

The Finance Committee had agreed to make up the earnings of those in distress to 1s 9d for the week, a total cost of £392 13s. During the meeting Revd W Thoresby proposed a motion, seconded by Sir JPK Shuttleworth, *'who in his usual cogent manner shewed the necessity of the proposed rise'*. Each household would receive a given amount according to the number in the family. *'1 person 3s.; a family of 2 persons, 5s.; of 3, 6s. 3d.; of 4, 8s.; of 5, 9s. 9d.; of 6, 11s. 6d.; of 7, 13s.; of 8, 14s. 6d.'*

The Central Executive Committee in Manchester had sent a grant of £900 for blankets and clothing. Sir JPK Shuttleworth urged that they lost no time in dispensing this grant; it should all be used for the purpose and sent out by the end of the month. This gentleman had already directed that the blankets be purchased from Rochdale and Manchester much to the dissatisfaction of the local suppliers, who had been hoping to make a handsome profit. Due to his astuteness the blankets had cost £344 3s 2d less 2½% discount; tenders had been received for the supply of clogs.

The Soup Committee reported they would be able to adapt the Mechanics Institution and would seek practical advice from other local soup kitchens. Sir James recommended they could get the best advice from a gentleman in Manchester who had visited the Glasgow soup kitchens. Did William and his family ever queue up for the soup kitchen I wonder to eke out their weekly 14s. 6d? Or had William senior's position in the warehouse made it possible for him to secure work?

Let us find out more about this influential gentleman, Sir JPK Shuttleworth.

James Phillips Kay-Shuttleworth, Educationalist

Burnley's own benefactor, Sir James Kay-Shuttleworth, was born James Kay into a Lancashire mill-owning family in Rochdale in 1804. He acquired the Shuttleworth appendage on his marriage in 1842 to Lady Jane Shuttleworth, heiress of Gawthorpe Hall near Burnley; he was made a baronet in 1849. They had four sons and a daughter, Sir Ughtred James Kay-Shuttleworth became an MP and was elevated as a baron in 1902.

James had qualified as a doctor in Edinburgh and worked among the poor of Manchester before becoming a civil servant. As Assistant Poor Law Commissioner he published a report in 1839 on 'The Training of Pauper Children'. That same year he had been appointed Assistant Secretary to the government's Committee of the Privy Council on Education. He was chief founder of the English system of publicly funded elementary education and founder of the first teacher training establishment, Battersea College, London. Due to ill health (he suffered from epilepsy) he retired from government in 1848.

He kept alive his passion for educating the poor by encouraging wealthy people in the Burnley area to fund schools. Amongst this group were father and son, John and Henry Moore, owners of Parsonage Mill. They set up a group of Church of England Schools, Revd Arthur Townley-Porter, Vicar of St Peter's Church and Revd Hugh Stamer of St James' Church were both keen supporters. During the cotton famine he acted as Vice-Chairman of the Manchester Central Relief Committee under Lord Derby, which accounts for his authority on the Burnley Relief Committee.

He had established the training college for teachers at Battersea in 1839 and had the government set up a national pupil-teacher system whereby the pupil-teachers taught throughout the school day and were themselves taught by the headmaster before or after school. This was a five-year programme with examinations and successful candidates would receive their certificate which would enable them to go on to further training should they so wish. This was the model that was later taken up in Scarborough.

Obviously William Ascough chose this course, possibly sponsored by the Moores, owners of Parsonage Mill, or even by Revd Hugh Stamer. The Clergy of the Parish, Headmaster, teachers and pupils of St James' School presented him with a 'very superior watch' before he set off for St Bede's College, Durham where he qualified with flying colours.

William Ascough in Derbyshire

At the age of 21 William took up his first teaching post in March 1869 as headmaster of Mosborough Endowed School in Eckington, Derbyshire. With the passing of the 1870 Education Act, the Eckington School Board was formed and William was appointed as its Clerk, in addition to his teaching commitments. Eckington included the townships of Mosborough, Renishaw, Killamarsh and Troway and one of his main achievements as Clerk was to have five large modern schools built in the area.

He took charge as first master of the largest, Eckington Board School. From the school record on the first day, 4 January 1875, we read that he favoured organising the children in their proper standards rather than by the monitorial system. He had a total of 135 children with more expected the following week. He also recorded that the Chairman, Vice-Chairman and another member of the Board had visited the school then he had taught the children a school song. William had used the services of one of the most eminent architects of the day, Mr E R Robson, with whom he became friends and later appointed as architect to oversee the Municipal School in Scarborough.

William had married his cousin, Ellen Ascough, in 1872. Her family had also moved from Hunton to find work but they had chosen the woollen mills of Bradford. After the death of both her father and brother, Ellen and her mother spent some time in Tasmania but returned to Bradford where Ellen had worked as a worsted weaver. William and Ellen's first two children died in infancy in the cold school house in Mosborough but Annie, born in 1876, and William born the following year in Eckington both survived. They all came to live at 13 West Grove Terrace, Falsgrave where Ethel completed the family in 1881.

The Sitwell Family

Among the people William met in Eckington was Lady Louisa Lucy Sitwell of Renishaw Hall. In 1817 Sir George Sitwell had the school house built and by 1831, Lady Sitwell was supporting a school for girls in Renishaw, which was also a Sunday School. The family had been the principal iron traders in the country and Eckington became the world centre for trading in nails. Sir Sitwell Sitwell received the

Baronetcy in 1808 from the Prince Regent, later to become George IV, because he had built an extension to his house in honour of the Prince's visit.

Since 1774, the Sitwell family had been spending the summer season in Scarborough. When they fell on hard times following the death of her husband, Sir Reresby Sitwell in 1862, Lady Louisa settled her family, Florence and George, permanently at the seaside. Their first house was at Sunnyside near Royal Crescent but they moved in 1870 to Woodend in the Crescent, next door to Londesborough Lodge. In 1886 George married Lady Ida Denison, daughter of Lord Londesborough.

The Royal connection continued as the Prince of Wales, later to become Edward VII, often stayed at Londesborough Lodge. Somewhat unfortunately this was where he contacted typhoid fever; as a result, Queen Victoria never visited Scarborough because it had almost taken the life of her beloved son. Sir George and Lady Ida produced three children, Edith, Osbert and Sacheverel, all renowned writers, while Sir George Sitwell became MP for Scarborough from 1882 to 1885 and again from 1892 to 1895.

Lady Louisa continued her good works by founding a 'House of Hope' for reclaiming and employing 'fallen girls' in Red House, a fine property in Sitwell Street, Falsgrave. Her granddaughter, Edith, was very disparaging about it, even suggesting that these 'unfortunates' had been kidnapped off the street and put to work 'tearing up our laundry'. The house was still in use in 1911, it closed in 1914. She also bought a house 'Hay Brow' in Scalby as a place of relaxation for Anglican clergy. In her later years Lady Louisa Sitwell moved to The Langtry Manor in Bournemouth, which had previously been known as Red House, where she died on 31 October 1911.

Could William Ascough's connection with the Sitwell Family in Renishaw have influenced him in applying for the post of Clerk to the Scarborough School Board?

William Ascough and the Scarborough School Board

The minutes of the Special Meeting of the Scarborough School Board held in the Town Hall on 14 January 1879 recorded in exquisite copperplate handwriting that those present included William Rowntree Esquire, Chairman of the Board; Alderman Porrett, Vice Chairman; Revd W C Dowding; Revd A G Riddell; Revd R Balgarnie; Mr Henry M Cross; Councillor W Barry; Revd R H Parr and Councillor R H Peacock. William Ascough had been called for interview on 7 January when the same members, sitting as the Committee of the Whole Board, had resolved: *That Mr Ascough be recommended to the Board for appointment as Clerk.*

When it was put to the vote the following week, however, Revd Dowding voted against, Mr Cross did not vote, Revd Balgarnie's vote was not recorded and the other six voted in favour. John Woodall Woodall had just taken over as Treasurer on the death of his father, John Woodall Esq.

Who were the illustrious gentlemen now on the Scarborough School Board? William Rowntree, born in 1806 at Low Mill, Pickering, set up the Drapers Store which was then in Newborough. Alderman George Porrett, born in 1818, ran a Chemist and Druggist shop, he was Mayor in 1875. Revd W C Dowding, born 1819, was the Church of England Vicar at St Thomas' Church, on East Sandgate, currently used by the Scarborough Sea Cadets; he was a widower with four children who were looked after by his sister. Revd A G Riddell, born in 1837, was the Roman Catholic Priest who, the following year, became Bishop of Northampton. Revd R Balgarnie, born 1826, was the Minister at Bar Street Congregational Church and St Andrew's Church on South Cliff, he had been appointed to the Board following the death of Revd James Mules.

Mr Henry Merry Cross, born 1831, originally lived in Scalby but now lived near the Workhouse on Dean Street (later Dean Road). He was a Collector of the Poor Rate and Assistant Overseer, who had been trained in public work, having spent some four years in London. The journalist who wrote 'The Scarborough Magazine' felt that although he objected to the Established Church on principle, he would still make a good Mayor in 1895. Councillor William Barry JP, born in 1828, manufactured bricks, tiles and stone, he lived in Royal Crescent Lodge and became Mayor in 1882. Revd Robert Henning Parr, born 1827, was the Church of England Vicar at St Martin's, South Cliff and finally Councillor Richard Hopper Peacock, born 1830, was an ironmonger, whitesmith and tinsmith living at 11 Westborough. William had joined a varied group of men from differing walks of life, with differing doctrines and politics.

Falsgrave was expanding rapidly by the time William arrived, the Board Schools were becoming overcrowded but Thomas S Aldis, HMI for the Harrogate District of Yorkshire, which included Scarborough, was on the case. Mr Aldis had been born in Surrey in 1844, the son of a Baptist Minister, now he and his wife Clara had three daughters and a son all under the age of nine. HMI Aldis had visited Falsgrave Board School on 16 January 1878 together with the members of the board.

In his report to the Lords of the Committee of Council on Education, dated 2 November 1879, he did not mince his words. He had investigated the reasons behind the facts, as shown by his comments on the school buildings in his area, in so far as they affected school attendance:

'They are too lofty to be well warmed or ventilated. While the walls are 20 inches thick the roof is but a double slate and an inch of lath and plaster. In summer the perpendicular rays of the mid-day sun

strike through it, in winter the chilled air streams down from it.'

He gave the comparative figures for school attendance: of the 6,266 children of school age living in Scarborough, there was an average attendance of 3,924 (63%). That would indicate that Scarborough now had over two thousand children who, rather than attend school, would be working for their families or roaming the streets. The child population had almost doubled since 1874 as had the truancy problem. Scarborough was not the worst, Pickering and Helmsley had 62% while Wetherby had only 58% attending school; Easingwold was the best with 79% attendance. In mitigation, Scarborough had almost twice as many children as Malton, the next highest population, and Helmsley had a total of only 840 children.

His observation on the actual teaching:

'a good teacher will teach well what he knows and a bad teacher ill.'

He felt particularly strongly about Infant Schools, he thought formal instruction in reading, writing and arithmetic started too early.

'Saddest of all, the child's right to the innocent enjoyment of life seems in most cases undreamed of... The youngest child, who needs the tenderest handling is entrusted to the rawest monitor...too frequently the lower half of the school is busy stupefying the wits which the other half is trying to quicken.'

The report shows that Scarborough was an important centre of population in the far-reaching but sparsely populated Harrogate District of Yorkshire. Obviously there was room for improvement but Mr Aldis has given us a benchmark from which to measure William Ascough's attainments.

The School Board had moved from the Town Hall into new premises, *'the Large Room in the building known as the Old Savings Bank, King Street'* in the February before William took up his post. The first School Board minutes in his distinctive handwriting are dated 31 March 1879. He was to remain in that office until 1903 when the Scarborough School Board became the Scarborough Education Committee, whereupon he became their Secretary until his retirement in 1905. He was then elected to the Town Council and returned to the Education Committee in 1906, becoming its Chairman. He held this position until his death in 1926 by which time he had served the cause of education in the borough for a total of 47 years. Before he took on the role of Chairman, he had served under four different chairmen, W S Rowntree for 4 years, Meredith T Whittaker for 12 years, John Stephenson for 3 years and Captain E T C Bower for 8 years. The next long serving member Revd Canon Dolan was on the committee for 23 years; Mr H M Cross had served for 18 years and John Stephenson for 17.

Of the total 50 members on the School Board, only two were female, Miss Florence Balgarnie, who followed her father in 1883, was instrumental in setting up cookery classes for the girls in all the Board Schools for six months each year with trained teachers from the Yorkshire School of Cookery. Miss Mary Catherine Dent, Gentlewoman of Raincliffe Villa, Valley Road, joined the board on 28 October 1901. She was a member of the Woodall family, born in 1857 at Ribstone Hall near Wetherby, the daughter of John Dent and his wife Mary Hebden Woodall.

The Balgarnies

Revd Robert Balgarnie came to Scarborough as Minister to Bar Street Congregational Church which had been opened in 1850. From the 1861 census we see he lived with his wife Martha and three daughters, Florence, Mary and Jessie in Victoria Street, next door to William Rowntree, Draper. It seems likely that Florence and William knew each other as children. At the age of 16, Robert, a Scot, had wanted to follow the Missionary, Robert Moffat, to Africa but decided to take up the position offered to him in Scarborough. In 1868 he transferred to the newly built St Andrew's Church on South Cliff sponsored by Sir Titus Salt of the Saltaire Woollen Mills and model factory village.

Even as a child, Titus Salt, born in 1803 near the West Riding town of Morley, had spent his holidays in Scarborough, initially on Merchants Row where he attended worship with his father at the 'Old Meeting House' in St Sepulchre Street. He contributed to the building of Bar Street Congregational Church and, with the development of South Cliff, he gave the money for the site as well as for the building of the new church. One year he brought all 2,000 of his workers to Scarborough, his favourite place, for the day. Following Sir Titus' death in 1877, Robert Balgarnie wrote a book 'Sir Titus Salt, Baronet: his life and its lessons'.

Revd Balgarnie was put on the School Board due to the sudden death of Revd James Mules. He had stood in the Triennial Election of 1874 but had narrowly lost out to Revd R H Parr of St Martin's Church, also on the South Cliff. He attended his first meeting on 25 June 1877 and on 26 January 1880, his final meeting he proposed that,

> 'The best thanks be given to W Rowntree and Alderman Porrett ... for discharging their duties as Chairman and Vice Chairman of the Board.'

It was seconded by Revd Parr.

Three years later his daughter Florence was elected to the School Board at the age of 26, the first woman on the Committee. William Rowntree had resigned and Meredith

Whittaker was elected as Chairman. Florence was very active in the National Society for Women's Suffrage, speaking on votes for women in the towns of the north. She wrote her letter of resignation on 25 April 1885 from 29 Parliament Street, London. John Stephenson, accountant of Belgrave Crescent, was duly elected to fill the vacancy.

Florence travelled round the United States in support of rights for women, including coloured women. She never married and in the 1911 census, she was living in Crouch End, London with her 86 year old mother, describing herself as a 'lecturer and journalist to the Women's Temperance Movement'. According to Elizabeth Crawford in her book 'The Women's Suffrage Movement' she died in a *pensione* in Florence in 1928, leaving £1,000 to endow a bed in Scarborough Hospital in memory of her parents.

More Board Schools

The School Board opened Falsgrave Boys' School in 1884. The competition for the plans for Gladstone Road Schools was won by the local firm of Messrs Hall and Tugwell with an innovative plan of light airy space with classrooms based around a central hall. In the girls' department there was a classroom equipped with a kitchen for Cookery and in the boys' section, a classroom for Science Instruction. It was opened by the Vice-President of the Committee of Council of Education, the Rt Hon A J Mundella on 7 June 1890. He was presented with a silver gilt key made by Bright's the Jewellers and expressed surprise at the high standard of work by Scarborough pupils exhibited in the classrooms.

The opening of the Friarage Schools on 28 February 1896 was far less ostentatious, Colonel Legard, Chairman of the Technical Institutes Committee of the North Riding County Council, officiated. An exhibition of pupils' work was on display for the public to view.

Scarborough School of Art

As for secondary education, in addition to the numerous private establishments both day and boarding, including the Ladies of St Mary's Convent in Queen Street, which opened its school in 1885, we have the Grammar School and the Government School of Art, otherwise known as the Art College. It had been promoted by the MP William Caine, and was first set up in Aberdeen Walk in 1882 under Albert Strange. He had had three years' experience as an art master at the School of Art in Liverpool, having trained at the Slade School in London. That same year he had had his first work accepted by the Royal Academy. Two years later he moved the school to Vernon Road into premises converted for the purpose from Harland's Baths.

Harland's Baths in Vernon Road with Christ Church in the background

Dr William Harland, Mayor of Scarborough in 1836, had established his 'warm water medicinal baths' here. He was the father of Edward James Harland who was born in Scarborough in 1831 before moving to Belfast to found the Harland and Wolff shipyard. Strange's establishment covered a full curriculum, it quickly gained a high reputation becoming one of the leading schools in the country.

> *'From the beginning the art school taught the National Course of Instruction for Government Schools of Art which consisted of separate courses in drawing, painting, modelling and design. Individual subjects included freehand and model drawing, geometry, perspective, still life, monochrome painting, oil and water colour painting and book illustration design, architecture, anatomy, and wallpaper and linoleum design.'*

Students from the college won national awards which brought in grants; two such students were sisters Edith and Ellen Robinson. The family had moved to Scarborough from Croyden where father, William, taught at the Quaker School. They came via Horton, Bradford to live in West Bank, Westbourne Grove with their mother, Maria, older brother Alfred and sister, Marian. The two younger girls attended the Art School between 1886 and 1891, Ellen apparently was one of only three students in the country to gain full marks in 'ornamental design' and in 1889 her design for a painted tile won a Royal Society of Arts Bronze Medal. Sister Edith married Nelson Dawson and moved to Chiswick where they were active in the Art and Craft movement producing pottery, metalwork and jewellery as well as painting. Edith wrote a book on 'Enamels' which was published in 1906.

Another student, Scarborough born Harry Wanlass, won a silver medal for oil painting and together with two others, had work shown at an Exhibition of British Art held in Budapest in 1898. He and his brother Charles continued to follow their artistic talents whilst also running the family painting and decorating business. In 1892, Alfred Strange made a proposal to the School Board to run a Branch Art Class for the pupil teachers. This was accepted: four representatives from the Board were elected to the Art School's governing body and Albert was paid the princely sum of £6.13s 4d a month.

He continued with his own painting as well as teaching and devising courses for the Elementary Schools; he was an illustrator of books, one such being J S Fletcher's 'A Picturesque History of Yorkshire'. Artistic communities thrived both in Scarborough and the fishing village of Staithes with his guidance; he was a keen yachtsman, as were many of his students. Apart from five years spent on his boat painting scenes in Brittany, he remained in Scarborough until his death in 1917. The school was bombed in the Second World War but the site is marked with a plaque.

The Muni

In order to give Scarborough's Board School scholars the opportunity of Secondary Education without overcrowding, the Committee came up with the idea of establishing a Higher Grade School. In July 1896 the School Board was authorised to borrow £5,000 through the Borough Corporation to buy a site from the North Eastern Railway Company on Plantation Hill, near the Valley Bridge. On 3 November that year they appointed E R Robson F S A of Palace Chambers, Westminster, with whom William Ascough had worked in Eckington, as Consulting Architect to draw up the Conditions of Competition.

From the 36 sets of plans submitted, that of the Scarborough firm, Messrs. Hall, Cooper and Davis, was selected. The 'Cooper' in the firm was one Thomas Edwin, born in Scarborough in 1874 and one time pupil at Central School. He was later to become Sir Thomas Edwin Cooper

RA FRIBA, a highly renowned architect whose buildings included the Star and Garter House at Richmond and the Port of London Authority Building. His mother had noticed his talent at an early age and had him apprenticed to John Hall and Frank Tugwell from 1885 until 1889.

The Muni

All was not plain sailing however, the Cockerton Report of 1898 prevented School Boards from spending money on higher education in spite of the scheme having been given approval earlier. They found a way round the government's ruling by giving charge of the school to the Town Council who could set up a Technical Instruction Committee and establish the school as a School of Science under the Technical Instruction Act of 1889, thus allowing it to levy rates for its maintenance.

Mr D W Bevan the Headmaster and the rest of the staff, many of whom were drawn from the Board Schools, were appointed on a temporary basis. Among the staff we find Miss Annie Ascough, daughter of William and one of the first monitors to be appointed at Gladstone Road School, and Mr Harry Norwood, from Killermarsh in Derbyshire. He was a prominent NUT member who was involved with the first NUT Conference to be held in Scarborough in 1906. He was destined to go on to higher things, first as Clerk to the Education Committee in Northallerton and later to a similar post in Birmingham. Annie and Harry married at St Martin's Church on 23 May 1904 and eventually become the grandparents of David Moore.

On 25 November 1900 some 336 boys and girls from the upper classes in the Board Schools took their places at the Higher Grade School. As a compromise, it was run by a board consisting of nine members of the Town Council, many of whom had previously served on the School Board, and nine members of the School Board. Mr Alfred Samuel Tetley was appointed permanent Principal of the School of Science and Secondary School on 2 November 1901, better known as the Municipal School, or more affectionately 'The Muni'.

The School Board had the backing of Arthur Dyke Acland, Education Minister under Gladstone, who had come to live in Scarborough. To compensate for the lack of a grand opening, the first Speech Day in January 1903 was a prestigious affair with its presentation of prizes. In addition to the former members of the old School Board, Mr M T Whittaker, Mr W S Rowntree, Mr Sanderson and William Ascough, the North Riding Education Committee was represented by Sir William Worsley, Colonel Legard, Mr F A Tugwell and Mr S P Turnbull. The guest speakers were Canon Garrod, Principal of Ripon Training College and Chairman of the North Riding Higher Education Committee, Sir Michael Sadler, who had been the civil service head of the London Education Department, Sir Alfred Dale who was Vice-Chancellor of Liverpool University and Mr J L Paton, High Master of Manchester Grammar School. The Muni was aiming high.

The University Extension Society and Sir Arthur Herbert Dyke Acland.

There were already other educational opportunities on offer in Scarborough. In 1872 the University of Cambridge had initially set up the idea of extending university level courses to people who would not normally be able to attend university. Gradually the universities of Oxford and London joined in and societies developed around the country. Top university lecturers gave courses for 10 to 12 weeks with the option of an examination at the end, funding was available. William and Joshua Rowntree were the founders of the Scarborough branch in 1879, together with Miss Theedham who ran Haddo House School in Brunswick Terrace; Florence Balgarnie was their first secretary.

Its early members included Archdeacon Blunt, Vicar of Scarborough, Revd Balgarnie and John W Woodall; Sir Harcourt Johnston, who became Lord Derwent, was its President. The first lecture was delivered by Richard G Moulton and in the first fifty years 116 courses of lectures had been held in subjects as diverse as Science and Economics, Art, History and Literature. Its committee also consisted of representatives from the County Council, the Borough Council, the District Teachers' Association (NUT) and the School of Art. In 1893, the Board elected three representatives Revd Canon Dolan, Mr Crop and Mr Hastings Fowler.

Another notable person involved at national level was Sir Arthur Herbert Dyke Acland. He had been involved with the administration of the Oxford Extension Lectures from 1878 particularly in the industrial areas of the North of England. He was one of the wealthiest landowners in the country but, in spite of his family base being in Devon, Arthur became the Liberal MP for Rotherham from 1885 to 1899. He was Vice-President of the Council of Education under both Gladstone and Lord Rosebery. It is recorded that on returning from a tour of the continent, he watched an elderly gentleman in Zürich teaching 'half a dozen defective children'. On his return he set up special teaching for 'the feeble minded'.

Acland had introduced the 'Evening Continuation School Code' in 1893 which transformed the status of night schools and made way for a better system of adult education. He was also responsible for the Elementary Education (Blind and Deaf Children) Act that same year. He had been thinking of leaving Scarborough in 1895 following the death of his father but he and his wife Alice were still living at Westholme on Fulford Road on the 1901 census with their daughter Mabel and a resident nurse. Ill health had led him to apply for the Stewardship of the Manor of Northstead when he left Parliament in 1899.

Education Act 1902

The Education Act 1902, implemented by 1904, brought about the change to enable Borough Councils to provide higher grade education: Scarborough could now levy a penny in the pound rate for the purpose. The Act abolished the School Boards and set up Local Education Committees. The last meeting of the Scarborough School Board was held on 25 May 1903 and the first meeting of the Scarborough Education Committee was held on 12 June 1903.

The North Riding County Council also met in June 1903 to pass the resolution:

"That a Sub-Committee be appointed for Education other than Elementary for the Borough of Scarborough under Section 6 of the First Schedule Part A of the Education Act 1902."

The members of the Scarborough Education Committee comprised Alderman Sanderson as the Chairman, Councillors Stephenson, Pirie, Bland, J W Rowntree, Handcock, Taylor, W S Rowntree (son of William Rowntree who had been Chairman of the School Board) and W H Fowler. For the Westwood Municipal School governing body in addition to the Education Committee we find Mrs Morgan, Mayoress, Captain E T C Bower, Miss Dent, Revd Canon Dolan, Mr M Farquher, Mr Horsman, Ven Archdeacon Mackarness, Mr Joshua Rowntree, Mr J Stephenson, Mr J P Turnbull, Colonel Legard, Rt Hon A H D Acland, Mr F A Tugwell and Dr R Cuff. Perhaps this minute from the first meeting indicates who was in charge:

> *'in reply to the Board of Education Circular No 452 all official correspondence will be conducted through the Secretary (Mr Ascough)'*

At last the originators of the Muni, designed to offer higher grade education to the children of Scarborough, were now legally permitted to follow their principles. They also had control of St Martin's Grammar School, the School of Art and the Evening Continuation Classes. The County Council gave £1,100 from their Treasury Grant and Colonel Legard referred to Scarborough as *"the beacon light in the rural darkness"*. The Rt Hon Arthur Dyke Acland held the office of Chairman of the Higher Education Sub Committee.

Moving on

We now have the background to the development of education in Scarborough. We have moved from the hit and miss chances offered to the children of the privileged and those 'deserving poor' in charitable institutions, to free education for all. We have also had a taste of politics preferring to control the masses by depriving them of higher grade opportunities rather than raising their skills and ambitions. We have met some interesting people from all walks of life who have in some measure, influenced the development of education in Scarborough and further afield. Now Secondary Education is on offer, but how were 'the deserving poor' to pay the fees?

William Ascough had already devised a plan. He had started at the very bottom and, through the benevolence he was fortunate enough to receive, made it to a position of great influence. He would now ensure that all children in his charge would similarly be given the opportunity to achieve through education.

*

PART FOUR
Scarborough United Scholarships Foundation

The Scheme of 1888

The marriage of the two charities, the Grammar School Trust and the Falsgrave Town Trust was brokered by the Charity Commissioners when they issued Scheme 872, approved by Her Majesty Queen Victoria, on 17 May 1888 and took place at a meeting of the Scarborough School Board eleven days later. Thus the Scarborough United Scholarships Foundation (SUSF) came into being.

Falsgrave Town Trust's dowry contained the fields Oxcliffe, Bell Corner, Quarry Bank, Fountain's Field and Land let to the North Eastern Railway together with the balance in hand of £253.12s. 3d and a Corporation Mortgage Bond. It came with the condition that *'an Award dated 24 March 1775, made under an Act of Parliament (15 George 3)'* (referring to the dividing and inclosing of the open commons and waste grounds within the manor and township of Walsgrave, otherwise known as Falsgrave) *'will not be affected by this Scheme.'* As for that of the Grammar School Trust, the £150 wrenched from the Corporation in 1851 was yielding an annual income of £15 by 1865 which had been paid to a private schoolmaster on condition that he gave instruction to four scholars.

It had been a protracted engagement; the Charity Commissioners wrote to the School Board in January 1886, sending copies of a 'Draft Scheme for the Grammar School Endorsements and Falsgrave Town Trust'. The Board agreed to their request to nominate two governors. On 27 June 1887, the Charity Commissioners informed the Board that the Scheme for the future administration of the Grammar School and the Falsgrave Town Trust had been duly approved by the Commissioners and submitted to the Education Department. Finally, in the Scarborough School Board minutes of 28 May 1888 we read:

> *'The Clerk reported that the Scheme for administration of the Charities known as "Scarborough Grammar School" and "The Falsgrave Town Trust" had been approved by Her Majesty in Council on 17 May 1888. The Charities were to be named the "Scarborough United Scholarships Foundation" and were to be administered by Nine Governors, of whom two were to be selected from the School Board.'*
>
> *It was unanimously resolved that the Chairman and Vice Chairman (Messrs. M T Whittaker and J Rowntree) be and are hereby elected as Governors of the Scarborough United Scholarships Foundation for the ensuing five years.'*

The nine trustees on the Management Board had an annual income of around £110 to manage. They were The Mayor of Scarborough for the time being, ex-officio, in 1888 Leasowe Walker Esq. who had been a solicitor in Tadcaster, held the office; one by the Vicar and Churchwardens of the parish church of Scarborough, Archdeacon Blunt, he was elected Chairman; William Ascough stood for the Elementary Schools; Meredith Whittaker and John Rowntree represented the School Board, Mr Rowntree was also the Treasurer; Alfred Peacock, Ironmonger, represented the Town Council and the three Falsgrave Freeholders were John Featherstone, James Bland and George Pullon who was also the Secretary. Was it mere coincidence that when the Ascoughs first moved to Scarborough they lived next-door to the Pullon family in Falsgrave?

In February 1889, four boys were accepted at St Martin's Grammar School at an annual fee of £5 each, which included books. In December that year the School of Art agreed to take Foundation Scholars for evening classes at a rate of fifteen shillings each. It took another two years before two girls were awarded scholarships to Mrs Raven's Girls' School but from then on both boys and girls were included. For about seven years the Governors held competitive examinations to decide to whom the scholarships should be awarded then they decided that, as the North Riding County Council was awarding scholarships, SUSF would give theirs to the unsuccessful scholars next in order of merit.

The Bishop of Hull, presiding at the SUSF presentation ceremony, gave a résumé of their first ten years. Dr Blunt, elevated to the newly re-ordered bishopric of Hull in 1891, had been the Vicar of St Mary's from 1864. As well as having been their first Chairman, he also subscribed to the Amicable Society, had helped to draw up their rules in 1866 and regularly attended their Annual Dinner, so he had first-hand knowledge of the children's charities, the town and its education.

He recalled that in this period scholarships had been awarded to 39 boys, 23 from Board Schools and 16 from Voluntary Schools, and 21 girls, 14 from Board Schools and 7 from Voluntary Schools. Of these, 26 boys and 20 girls had gained distinction in examinations held in connection with the College of Preceptors and the Cambridge Local Examinations. All the boys had gained certificates from the Science and Art Department in mathematics and in organic chemistry. Degrees at the Victoria University had been awarded to three boys, one in 1895, one in 1896 and yet another in 1897; a further one was expected in 1898. There is no mention of any girl making it to university in this period. And so the charity remained unchanged for fourteen years.

Scarborough School Board Scholarships and Prizes

It is possible that William Ascough drafted the SUSF's constitution based on his own experience. He had been well enough educated to become a pupil teacher in a school provided by the Church in Burnley, namely St James' under their Vicar, Revd Hugh Stamer, and had been awarded a scholarship. As Clerk to the School Board, William encouraged the members to provide scholarships and grants so that others too would be able to take advantage of what was on offer in order to better their position in life. In Scarborough he tried, without success, to have presentations of prizes as had happened in Burnley; instead awards were confined within the schools but publicity was given through the local papers. Chairman of the Board Meredith Whittaker, journalist with the 'Scarborough Mercury', School Board member since 1880, owner of the 'Evening News' from 1882, was well placed to do this.

Prizes to encourage pupils' learning had started before William Ascough came to Scarborough but he developed it further. Attendance cards were used in schools and prizes given for punctuality and good attendance. Lord Derwent, otherwise known as Sir Harcourt Johnstone, Scarborough's MP from 1869 to 1880, awarded the Lancasterian History Prize annually. Prizes from the Taylor Trust were also awarded at the Lancasterian School. The minutes of 25 November 1878 state that, following the sale of the Girls' School of Industry for the sum of £750, scholarships of £10 each would be awarded to three girls each year, providing they stay at school to the age of 15, the criteria was based on:

'a) plain sewing, designing and cutting out and making garments.

b) the most intelligent and practical knowledge of domestic economy applicable either at home or in service'

The School of Industry in Cook's Row had been started in 1808 by 'the ladies of Scarborough' and, according to Solomon Wilkinson Theakston in his 'Guide to Scarborough,' in 1854 about seventy girls attended:

'who receive instruction not only adapted to raise their moral character, but to fit them for the domestic circle in which they will probably move.'

In June 1883 Miss Augusta Woodall and Mrs Joshua Rowntree agreed to be the examiners for these scholarships but Mrs R H Tindall *'regretted she would not be at home'*. Two years earlier, Mrs Aldis had been the examiner and her husband the HMI agreed to award the scholarships. Miss Woodhead of Westlands was to award marks for Needlecraft on 28 May 1888, which would indicate there was cooperation among the Scarborough schools in both the voluntary and private sectors. It would appear that William Ascough invited Lord Derwent to award the prizes or failing that, the Mayor or even Sir George Sitwell but without success.

In 1880 Mr Wheater, owner of a boarding school at 33 Albermarle Crescent, which he described as 'the Grammar School', marked the Johnstone Lancastrian History Prize and awarded 192 marks out of a possible 200 to the winner. No names are recorded but he complimented the students on the neatness of their handwriting and their industrious application to the historical period. Charles Laughton, who was to become a famous actor of stage and screen, had attended this establishment but was hastily removed when his parents learned he had suffered a beating from the headmaster.

An interesting minute from 13 June 1887 tells that Mr Raven, Headmaster of St Martin's Grammar School, had examined the Science and Art Scholarships on the subject 'Magnetism and Electricity' awarding equal first prize to W C Lott and W L Ascough with 78 marks each. Sadly

William's son, William L, born in Eckington and now aged 11, died the following October from cancer of the spleen.

The School Board supported Pupil Teachers, thus also benefitting the children they taught, by holding classes during the summer holidays. A person of particular interest to my family, Albert E Morley, appears in the minutes dated 10 October 1887 as a pupil teacher in his first year who was to be transferred from Falsgrave School to the Lancasterian Boys' School. He is mentioned again on 3 October 1892 in a list of teachers who had qualified as assistants at the recent Queen's Scholarship examinations and been appointed as teachers. The men were on a salary of £50 per annum and the women £40. Grandfather Albert Morley, born in 1873, the son of an innkeeper in Westborough and whose mother came from Dumple Street, took up his first post as a qualified teacher in Gladstone Road Boys' School before becoming the Headmaster of Friarage Boys' School in August 1919.

Courses of a practical nature were on offer to the public. We read from a report received from the County Council's Examiner on Technical Classes in November 1896,

> 'most of the pupils who passed the examinations did so with great credit to themselves and to their teachers.'

There were 66 students in the Cookery section comprising lodging-house keepers, girls at home and domestic servants: the benefit to some of these was that they could be promoted to plain cooks. There were only 8 students in the Laundry Class but 114 in Dressmaking; among these were married women, domestic servants, shop assistants and girls at home and as a result some would now be able to seek situations as lady's maids. Comment was made that they had passed the examination very successfully even though it had meant working late at night after a hard day at work.

Mr Underwood was in charge of classes held in the Friarage Schools in basic education, Reading, Writing and Composition; Arithmetic; Lantern Lectures; Drill; Needlework; Cookery and Singing. In 1903 Robert Underwood was appointed assistant secretary to the Scarborough Education Committee (successor to the School Board) and subsequently succeeded the retiring William Ascough as Secretary in 1905.

The Scarborough School of Art offered Art Tuition; Physiography; Practical, Plane and Solid Geometry; Geometrical Drawing; Inorganic Chemistry; Hygiene and Human Physiology. The cost to students was 6 shillings, payable at 6d a week, or only five shillings for the whole course if paid at the start, or 2s 6d for just one subject; the students could get grants from the County Council. The cost of Art School courses ranged from £60 for Pupil Teachers on the Art Tuition Course to £15 for the Hygiene classes.

Staff and Pupil Teachers were given courses in First Aid by the St John Ambulance Society and were examined by Dr Gawler Murray in January 1898. Fifty Board School teachers of girls and infants and ten from other Voluntary Schools attended a series of lessons on Musical Drill in 1887. The School Board kept abreast of all things educational. When an International Congress on Technical Education was planned in Paris in August 1900, the board requested to receive the papers produced there for a fee of five shillings. Pupils from Central Boys' School sent exhibits to the Imperial Institute in London, which were then forwarded to the International Exhibition; they included a Venetian Ironwork Screen, a Map of Australia, a Shaded Drawing of the Virgin and Pen and Ink Studies of Animals.

The Whittaker Family

Meredith Thompson Whittaker had joined the School Board at its fourth Triennial Election in 1880, he had been promoted to Vice Chairman and on the retirement of William

Rowntree, he was elected Chairman on 5 February 1883. He held the chairmanship until ill health forced him to retire in 1895. Meredith's father, Thomas Whittaker, was a deeply religious temperance missionary who had held audiences spellbound at rallies in London. He came from a farmstead on the Yorkshire borders near Clitheroe and in his youth had worked long hours as a dresser in a factory in Blackburn where he became aware of the damage caused to his fellow workers by the 'demon drink'.

When he settled in Scarborough in 1849 he ran a Temperance Hotel in Newborough; he was elected to the Council and became Mayor in 1880. His two sons, Meredith born in 1841 and Thomas Palmer, born eight years later, set up in business as iron mongers in Westborough, with an iron foundry in Vine Street.

Their father had been an avid contributor to the local papers and in 1875 they became associated with the 'Scarborough Mercury' and its off-shoot the 'Evening News' which Meredith opened in 1882. He was elected to the Council in 1886 and was made a JP in 1894. He was Mayor of Scarborough for two terms, from 1919 until 1921. Meredith was a member of the Liberal Party, at the Radical end, and was instrumental in the building of their magnificent new premises in Westborough, opened by the retiring Prime Minister, Lord Rosebery in 1895. The building bears that name for its present function as a Wetherspoon pub, after serving as a medical centre during the war and then as the co-operative store, Unity House.

His brother Thomas Palmer, who had been editor of 'The Mercury', took on the ironmongery business and in 1892 became MP for the Spen Valley. Meredith married Kitty, they had three daughters and one son, Francis Croydon. Francis followed his father into both the business and the Town Council where he too served two terms as Mayor from 1934 to 1936. He named his son Meredith, born in 1914 and this Meredith Whittaker continued the Scarborough Evening News, which achieved its centenary under his directorship. When he died in 1984 the business was sold to Johnston Press PLC: today it exists as a local weekly paper, the Scarborough News.

Under the first Meredith Whittaker's Chairmanship, William Ascough and the School Board made great progress. The number of children on their school registers was 1,891 in the year 1880 and by the time he left the Board in 1895, they had 3,999 pupils, many having moved from other schools. He also donated an annual scholarship to the Board School pupils. Now, with the blessing of Her Majesty Queen Victoria, they had a means of helping the poorer children in the town to achieve greater things through the SUSF.

SUSF amalgamates with the Amicable Society

After some four years of wrangling, the Governors of the SUSF and the members of the Amicable Society Committee eventually agreed to amalgamate; the official scheme was drawn up as follows under the aegis of the Board of Education.

> 'Sealed on 20 June 1904 between
> 1) The Scarborough United Scholarships Foundation regulated in 1888 and
> 2) The Scarborough Amicable Society founded in 1729.
> The Governing Body... shall when complete... consist of 13 persons:
> ONE Ex-officio being the Mayor of Scarborough
> TWELVE Representative Governors appointed for the term of three years:
> Three by the Town Council of the Borough of Scarborough through its Education Committee;
> One by the Yorkshire North Riding County Council acting through its Education Committee;

One by the Vicar and Churchwardens of the Parish of Scarborough;
One by an electing body consisting of the Managers of such Public Elementary Schools in the Borough of Scarborough as are not provided by the Local Education Authority ; and
Not more than six subscribers of the Scarborough Amicable Society. The number of Governors appointed shall be at the rate of one for every 15 subscribers.
A representative Governor need not be a member of the appointing body.'

It lists various points: religious opinions or lack of shall not affect qualification; a quorum needs five governors and the Chairman shall have a casting vote in case of equality of votes.

'The Application of Income
After payment of the expenses of administration, the yearly income of the Foundation shall be applied by the Governors in maintaining
A) Exhibitions tenable at
  1) any Public Secondary School; or
  2) an Institution of technical, professional, or industrial instruction approved by the Governors for a period of three years which may be extended...
to be awarded as nearly as possible equally between boys and girls, whose parents are bona fide resident in the Borough of Scarborough and who
  a) have for not less than three years been scholars in a Public Elementary School in the Borough of Scarborough, or
  b) are orphans or have lost one parent and have become reduced by misfortune from better circumstances ... to those in need of pecuniary assistance, a payment of not more than £10 a year

B) not less than two Exhibitions, each of a yearly value of not less than £40 nor more than £80 tenable at any University or Institution of higher education approved by the Governors...

with the same conditions but adding

In the case of scholars with exceptional merit who are intending to proceed to the Universities of Oxford or Cambridge the amount of the Exhibition may be increased to such extent as the Governors think fit.'

The Exhibitions, to be held for three years, were to be competed for openly and only awarded if the candidate was 'adjudged worthy'; they could be taken away for misconduct or idleness. The competitive element was ruled out in 1909 for Public Secondary School places but was retained for scholarships to the Graham Sea Training School until 1927. University and Post Secondary Exhibitions were competed for until 1946.

The assets listed in the First Schedule were:

UNITED SCHOLARSHIPS FOUNDATION
  Personal Estate
  Consols £484 9s 2d gross yearly income £12 2s.0d
  Local Loans Stock £4,609 9s 3d
    do   £138 5s 9d

AMICABLE SOCIETY, INCLUDING THE COCK HILL CLOSE CHARITY
  Real Estate
  School and House gross yearly income £40. 0s 0d
  Personal Estate
  Bank of England Stock £2,221 13s 4d
    do   £234 18s 2d (in 1803)

The six Governors elected from the Amicable Society were Messrs. W Ascough, now living at 63 Trafalgar Square; George Lord Beeforth of Belvedere; Henry Chapman, Chemist, 52 Newborough Street; Richard Smith, Jeweller, 13 Albermarle Crescent; John Stephenson, Accountant, 44 Esplanade Road and Thomas Francis Taylor, Confectioner, 5 Park Avenue. H E Donner was the Secretary and the Mayor in 1904 was William Morgan, husband of Octavia Flora Morgan, who became President of the Amicable Society in 1904. Councillor William Morgan was Mayor from 1902 to 1905, followed by William Hastings Fowler and in 1906, John W Rowntree. Revd T E Lindsay had followed Dr Blunt as Vicar of St Mary's from 1905 to 1913. Also on the committee were Ven Archdeacon Mackarness of St Martin's Church, William Sanderson, Schoolmaster, of 'Roseberry' in Fulford Road; George Handcock, Surgeon, of 6 Westfield Terrace; Meredith Whittaker, Journalist, 28 Albermarle Crescent and Frank Alfred Tugwell, Architect, of 'Wyndcliff' on Holbeck Hill. The Amicable School and two dwelling houses were sold on 13 February 1906 and the money invested to bring in income.

The first Exhibition was awarded in 1905 to David Gilchrist enabling him to study at Leeds University 'with a view to qualifying as a Mining Engineer.' In 1906 *'none of the competitors shewed sufficient merit to justify the Scholarship being granted'* although Frederick Northorp received £20 for attending Cambridge University. The next year saw the first girl, Ida Garton, enter for an Arts Course and James Hill for one in Science, both at Leeds University. In 1906 thirteen Secondary Exhibitions were awarded at the Municipal Secondary School and four at St Martin's Grammar School making a total of 30 boys and 17 girls with exhibitions at the Municipal School and 13 boys at the Grammar School, 60 students in all who otherwise would not have had a secondary school education. The amount paid annually for each pupil was £7 which covered tuition, books and examination fees.

One Special Scholarship for Girls had been given, it was intended for training at a special institution to thoroughly equip a girl for Domestic Service and also included tuition, board, lodging and an outfit on leaving the Institution. In addition, all the Old Scholars on the Amicable Foundation had been supplied with clothing 'as provided for in the Scheme of Amalgamation.' In later years many awards were made to students attending Teacher Training Colleges, maintenance awards were given to families to enable pupils to stay in secondary education an extra year and in 1915 mention is made of three boys being awarded *'Exhibitions of £14 each to enable them to undertake a course of Sea Training.'*

William Ascough was elected Chairman of the SUSF in 1908 and remained on the committee until his death in July 1926; he was also President of the Amicable Society at the time. By 1926 the annual income had increased to £573 per annum. The nominal value of the University Scholarship had gone up to £80 and loans were also offered to a number of students *'which are in most cases duly repaid.'* A University Scholarship was awarded to Charles Leslie Harris; loans were given to enable a student to take an examination at Trinity House, Hull, he gained a Second Mate's Certificate. One student ventured abroad to take a course at Caen University while yet another was able to attend the Royal College of Art; a fourth continued his course at Cambridge University. Grants were given to two students, one at Leeds University and the other at Leeds Training College.

In 1914 the six representatives of the Amicable Society were Messrs. Richard Smith, Harry Vasey, T F Taylor, A M Daniel, G Boothby and R Underwood. When the Amicable Society celebrated its 200th Anniversary in 1929, Mr Underwood combined the roles of President and Honorary Secretary as well as being a representative on the SUSF, the other Amicable Society representatives included Mr G W

Boothby, Mr A Gibson, Mr Mainsmith, Mr F G Pexton and Mr G K G Pindar.

On 9 July that same year joining these six members on the SUSF Committee we find Mr G W Boothby as Chairman and Mr G Mainsmith as Vice-Chairman; Councillor Abraham Moore, the Mayor; Alderman J W Butler, Councillor Merryweather and Mrs Lily Birdsall were the three members appointed by the Town Council Education Committee; F A Tugwell Esq. J P, by the North Riding County Council Education Committee; Revd J W Capron by St Mary's Church and finally Captain Preston Cobb represented the schools not provided for by the Local Education Authority.

The Mechanics Institute

At their meeting on 2 December 1960, the SUSF committee resolved to accept the funds following the closure of the Scarborough Mechanics and Literary Trust. The sum involved amounted to approximately £500, so long as they could be merged unconditionally with the Foundation. S D McCloy was Clerk, Miss L A Drew was in the Chair, Canon D Oxby Parker, Mrs L C Harland, Mrs M L Priestly, Alderman M E Bird, Mr C H Bradley, Mr A C Morley, Mr J S Rawling and Mr E Moore were in attendance and Mr G C Nock the Divisional Education Officer was also present.

The first Mechanics Institute had been set up in Edinburgh in 1821, Liverpool and London followed suit in 1823 before spreading to towns and cities all round the country including Scarborough. The movement revolutionised access for ordinary people to education in the sciences and technology. An 1834 publication 'The Printing Machine: Or a Companion to the Library' informs us that the Scarborough Mechanics Institute had held its Annual General Meeting on 11 November. Sir George Cayley bart. MP, the Scarborough born pioneer of aviation and inventor of a prosthetic hand amongst other things, was in the Chair, the main discussion was around coming out of debt by the following year. Perhaps they were relying on two newly elected members, The High Sheriff of Yorkshire, Henry Preston of Moreby Hall and Sir Charles Styles, who followed Sir George as MP for Scarborough in 1837.

On the subject of Mechanics Institutes generally, an article in the magazine suggests their success was due to

'not only the mere attraction of novelty but ... an ardent desire to obtain useful and solid information...
The prosperity of the country must be greatly advanced by improving the general intelligence of our artisans.'

Plaque on the Library also identifying the Mechanics Institute

The room in Newborough Street became too small for the number of people wishing to better themselves and in 1851 they moved into 'the building formerly known as the Odd Fellows Hall' in Vernon Road, which in 1930 became The Public Library. Theakston's 'Guide' informs us that there were *'occasional lectures occasionally delivered by friends of the Institute'* and regular courses in the evenings of the winter months which included reading, writing, arithmetic, drawing and modelling, all well attended. Their library contained upwards of a thousand 'well selected' volumes and the reading room was well supplied with periodicals. To defray costs they sub-let the large room for public occasions.

Jack Binns tell us that Dr Peter Murray, to whom Theakston dedicated his 'Guide' and who practised medicine in Scarborough from 1827 to 1864, was a founder member of the Mechanics Institute. He set up a charitable outpatient hospital in this Vernon Road building in 1851and also provided annual suppers for the cab drivers and their wives. In Bulmer's Directory of 1890 we find that A E Hick was its President, Henry Merry Cross of the School Board and C Webb were honorary secretaries; the resident librarian was Alfred Linskill. At one time John Woodall was the President, J Hest and Michael Hick were vice-presidents, John Leckenby was Treasurer and the two secretaries were John Edmund and Samuel Bayley.

An interesting document dated 10 January 1930 witnesses the formation of:

'an Unincorporated Charitable Institution to be known as '"The Scarborough Mechanics and Literary Trust" to commemorate for all time the Mechanics and Literary Institute which was founded in Scarborough on 12 November 1830 and was an acquisition to the town up to the date of its dissolution on 1 October 1929.'

This new organisation inherited £551.7s.11d to be distributed for the promotion of education in the Borough of Scarborough and to be administered by Trustees with an elected Chairman.

> 'Credited representatives of local educational institutions may be invited to the annual meetings of the Trustees with the object of stimulating interest in the Charity and raising funds to augment the capital thereof.'

The final clause mentions that if the Trustees find it *'expedient to put an end to the Charity'* any remaining funds should be given to *'such institution or institutions connected with education as the Trustees shall determine'*. It was drawn up by C W Moody, Solicitor; signed, sealed and delivered by Sir Meredith Thompson Whittaker, Knight (grandson of the Chairman of the Scarborough School Board), George Fawcett Gibson, Boarding House Proprietor; Charles Webb, Accountant; John Turton Sinfield, Tobacconist; Robert Cole, Accountant. Also signed, sealed and delivered in the presence of G F Mitchell, Solicitor with the same firm, by Frederick Dove, Sculptor, William Malton, Brick Manufacturer; Ann Butterworth and Alice Butterworth, Spinsters, all of Scarborough. SUSF obviously fitted their criteria.

Added Extras

Over the years various charities with connections to children and education have found a home with SUSF. In 1998 committee member Miss Hilda Briggs

> *'informed the Governors that steps were being taken to wind up three local charities:- the Glauert Memorial Fund, The Scarborough School Prize Fund and the Taylor Education Fund'.*

They were all duly transferred to the SUSF account as recorded in the minutes of 15 January 1999.

'Glauert Mathematics Prize Fund'

There were two separate funds in Miss Glauert's name, both unsurprisingly for Mathematics, her special subject. In 1945 on Miss Glauert's retirement from the Girls' High School, the Old Girls Club decided to raise funds to award an annual prize to a student who showed most potential in Mathematics. In 2015 the Old Girls Association, as the Club became known, approached the SUSF to administer their 'Glauert Mathematics Prize', awarded to a girl at the 6th Form College who was going to university to study mathematics. After much deliberation, the committee had to refuse on the grounds of its exclusivity, so it continues as the responsibility of the Old Girls' Association.

A second 'Glauert Memorial Mathematics Scholarship' fund came from a legacy in the will of Alexandra Trail dated 11 November 1960. This was to be given for the best result in 'O' level Mathematics, it was awarded from 1963 to 1967. In 1977 the Club sought the help of Miss Ida Slarke as to the whereabouts of this fund at which point the Charity Commission became involved. Miss Slarke had been the French Mistress at the Girls' High School, later Deputy Head and, on retirement, the first lady Mayor of Scarborough in 1972. It would seem that through the good offices of Miss Briggs, this was the fund that came to the SUSF. It is some indication of the esteem in which Miss Glauert was held that there were two funds raised in her name.

Miss Elsa Glauert was born in Ecclesall, Sheffield in 1882; she had two older brothers, Ludwig born in 1879 and Otto in 1881 followed by a younger sister Gertrud in 1883 and younger brother Hermann in 1892. Their Father, Johann Ernst Louis Henry Glauert was a naturalised British citizen; he had come from Germany and settled in Sheffield where he worked as a merchant and manufacturer of cutlery. His British wife, Amanda Watkinson, had also been born in Germany. Their children were extremely talented: Ludwig became a palaeontologist and emigrated to Australia. Hermann excelled at Cambridge as an astronomer and went into the newly emerging aeronautical industry at the Royal Aircraft Factory in Farnborough. He had a very untimely death in 1935 due to an accident involving the felling of a tree whilst he was out walking. Brother Otto opened Lisvane School in Scarborough in 1923, the year after Elsa took on the first Headship of the Girls' High School.

Elsa had won Sheffield's 'Earnshaw Scholarship' which enabled her to study mathematics at Girton College, Cambridge. In 1917 her name appears on the 'Official List of Registered Teachers' teaching at London's Clapham High School where she had completed her year's teacher training. An article was published in the Scarborough paper on 2 January 1947 commemorating her 40 years as a teacher; this included her time as the first Headmistress of the Girls' High School from 1922. It states that her ambition was:

'to turn out women of wide interests, interests extending beyond the school, and trained for the job that they would have to do – and that in most cases … is homemaking.'

Rather than suggesting that a woman's place should be in the home, she was being realistic. Whilst at Cambridge, she was an ardent Suffragist, she was keen on equal status for women and against the rule that women had to retire from teaching when they married. Many of her pupils became teachers and she also encouraged many to take up nursing, she kept in touch with her pupils through the 'Old Girls' Club'. Her comment may resonate with today's teachers some seventy years later:

'Being a schoolmistress ...is not what it was. Nowadays there is so much form-filling and rendering of returns that it distracts the mistress's interest from the only thing that really matters – the pupils.'

The newspaper article suggests that during her time at the Scarborough High School for Girls she had *'had a hand in shaping the careers and characters of some 1,500 girls.'*

Her wisdom and influence did not stop there as she was appointed governor to the High School for Boys, secretary of the Children's Hospital League and was on the committee for the Alice Brooke Home.

'Scarborough Schools Prize Fund'

The origins of this fund are more difficult to trace but it is most likely that it came from the prizes awarded by the original School Board. Less than six months after its inception, the Scarborough Education Committee looked into the scholarships and prizes for which they were responsible and reported in its minutes dated 24 November 1903,

(a) Johnstone Lancasterian History Scholarship

In 1874 Lord Derwent (then Sir Harcourt Johnstone Bart) to make the transfer of the Lancasterian Schools to the School Board, gave to the Scarborough School Board the sum of £125 the interest of such sum to be used yearly in the award of prizes to pupils of the Board Schools who showed the greatest proficiency in English History.

(b) The Domestic Economy Scholarships

In 1878 the Committee and Trustees of the "Girls' School of Industry" in unison with the Managers of a "Girls' School in Falsgrave", presented to the School Board the sum of £750 to fund Scholarships to be presented annually to the girls in the Board Schools who show
  (1) The greatest proficiency in plain sewing, darning and in cutting out and making garments; and
  (2) The most intelligent and practical knowledge of domestic economy applicable either at home or in service.

(c) Whittaker Testimonial Fund

In 1896 a portrait and a sum of £100 was presented to the School Board as a Testimonial of esteem to the late Chairman, M T Whittaker, Esq. J. P.
  The £100 was given for "Foundation of some Scholarship at the discretion of the Board."

It specifies how the monies are invested:

Mortgage Cliff Bridge Company @ 4% - £500.0s.0d
Do   (Corporation) @ 4% - £125.0s.0d
(Wardell)   @ 3¾%   £300.0s.0d
Monies in hand (uninvested)   £ 50.0s. 0d
                                  £975.0s.0d

The Committee agreed to award seven scholarships at £5 each to pupils from Board Schools by competitive examination, to attend the Higher Grade School pending the completion of its organisation. On consultation, Mr Whittaker suggested his prize be one of £100 invested with the Cliff Bridge Company, the pupil should remain in school for three years, being awarded £5 each year. If the money did not cover the award, he would consider amending the sum invested so the Scholarship would be £5 per annum. The committee accepted his offer.

'The Taylor Education Fund'

Again through Miss Briggs and at the same meeting, the Taylor Education Fund found its way into the SUSF. It had originally been set up by Joseph Taylor, a devout Quaker, to cover the costs of educating thirteen to fourteen poor boys in Scarborough in a school operating the Lancastrian system. The boys would change every two years. It would be administered by a group of trustees, two of whom would be Quakers. The requirements for the 'Taylor Trust Prize' were *'diligence, and good conduct with regular and punctual attendance.'*

Joseph left sums of money and the means of raising money in his will dated 4 May 1810. He devised income from lands for providing coal for the poor, when the land was sold in 1868 and 1870 the money was invested. We are told the dividends amounted to £41.7s.6d and were duly distributed. He gave £1,000 to construct a large house and keep it in repair with fourteen separate apartments on Cooks Row in 1817. It was to house rent free the Scarborough elderly and 'respectable' poor, preferably married but without families. The house was to be administered by the same trustees. A family member by the name of Mrs Hannah Mennell received £800.

Interestingly he and the Rowntrees did not see eye to eye even though they were all Quakers, he wrote a strong letter asking to know about money he had invested. A minute in the Education Committee meeting of 8 March 1905 noted that £100 of this trust was held in the Scarborough Gas Company; they requested that it should come under the Charitable Trusts Act.

'The Nessie Linn Memorial Trust Fund'

On 22 June 2000, Beryl R Waters, Secretary of The Soroptimists International of Scarborough, wrote to Mr Bob Bedford, secretary of SUSF, *'with a view to handing over the monies of the Nessie Linn Fund.'* The Soroptimists had decided at their meeting that *'the existing funds were inadequate to provide sufficient income for present day donations.'*

On 22 September the SUSF Governors agreed to accept the offer and on 19 May 2001, through Miss Dena Hebditch, at the time a member of both the Soroptimists and the SUSF Committee, £643.09 was credited to the account. Nessie Linn had died in 1978, in her will she had enlisted the help of the local Soroptimists to run The Nessie Linn Memorial Fund 'for the relief of the Poor and Needy' under the heading 'Culture and Arts'.

So who was Nessie Linn? If we go back to the 1861 census we find James Linn, born in 1820, living at 8 East Sand Gate as a Bookseller with his wife Jane, sons John and George and daughters Jane and Alice. Ten years later John, born in 1857, was a carver and gilder who, by 1901, was living with his wife Sarah at 26 Londesborough Road. Their eldest son, John, born in 1880, worked in a bank but the other sons, James Frederick, born in 1882, Henry, born 1885, and Charles, born in 1885, followed their father's profession. According to the Scarborough Directory of 1913, the Linn family ran a Fine Arts business with two premises, one at 20 Huntriss Row and the other at 54 Ramshill Road, the Old St Martin's Grammar School.

A painting of 'Beach Scene at Low Tide' by Henry Barlow Carter which was sold in 2009 by Tennants the Auctioneers was given the provenance:

'John Linn & Sons, 20 Huntriss Row & Old St Martin's Grammar School, Ramshill Road, Scarborough.'

We can tie it to earlier connections, Paul Marny, who taught Albert Strange, Head of the School of Art, came to live in Scarborough; David Fowler tells us in his 'Scarborough Snippets' that Marny sold most of his paintings to John Linn after 1878.

Nessie, whose maiden name was Mary Agnes Dodds, was born in 1892, her father, William Robert Dodds was a master mariner and they lived at 10 Mulgrave Terrace. They moved to Candler Street and Nessie worked in a jeweller's Shop. In 1915 she married Charles Linn, the youngest son of John Linn, proprietor of the business. Charles and Nessie had a son, John Charles, who rose to the rank of Captain in the Green Howards but was killed in 1944 and is buried in the Bayeux War Cemetery. Nessie ran a highly esteemed chocolate shop at 52A Ramshill Road for many years.

The Graham Family

The Maisie Graham Music Prize is mentioned in the Education Committee minutes dated 24 February 1923 and, although it may have no direct connection with SUSF, the Graham family played an important part in educating the children of Scarborough.

Christopher Colborne Graham had been born in the Camberwell area of London in 1857, his father was a Tea Dealer and land owner in Lambeth. In the 1891 Census he had moved to Hull where he was living with his wife, Mary, sons Christopher 6 and Hugh 2 and daughter Mary only 1 year old at 165 Beverley Road, West Sculcoates. His occupation is given as 'Secretary to Paint and Colour Company' although in the next census he is living in Ilkley as a 'retired Analytical Chemist'. Hull had a thriving paint industry with white lead imported from Holland, linseed from the Baltic and a well established trade in whale oil convenient for the factories on Bankside.

C C Graham moved to Scarborough and became Mayor of the Borough in 1913, he remained in office throughout the duration of the First World War, longer than any other Scarborough Mayor, relinquishing his place to Meredith Whittaker in 1919. His daughter Mary, known as Maisie, acted as his Mayoress. She had lived with her grandmother in Walton on Thames and in 1911 was staying in Queen Alexandra's House, Kensington Gore, while studying music. Miss Graham was made a life-member of the Amicable Society following donations during her time as Mayoress and served on the Committee; she was a warden from 1925 to 1926, resigning in February 1928. She kept an interest in the Society and when they put out an appeal for funds in 1930 she subscribed ten shillings.

The 1923 entry in the Education Committee Minute Book referred to a Music Prize donated by Maisie Graham. The first recipient was Eric Fenby and a second award of £5 was also given to him a few years later. According to the 1911 census, Eric William Fenby was born in 1906, his father was a gas fitter and the family lived in Candler Street. Apparently at the age of twelve he was the organist at Trinity Church. The life he might have been expected to lead without financial support from both this scholarship and a grant from SUSF, was far removed from what he was able to achieve.

Eric Fenby had heard that the great Bradford born composer, Frederick Delius, was no longer able to write his music due to illness and felt he could help. In 1928 Eric went to Grez-sur-Loing in France and offered himself as amanuensis; he stayed until Delius died in 1934. It was no easy task, Delius was blind and paralysed, but they eventually found a way of communicating. Among Delius' better known works are 'On hearing the first cuckoo in Spring' and 'A Village Romeo and Juliette'; with Eric's help he composed 'A song of Summer' among other works. In later life Eric Fenby was Director of Music at the North

Riding Training College in Scarborough and Professor of Harmony at the Royal Academy of Music.

As Mayor from 1914 to 1918, Councillor Graham was entitled to attend the Education Committee meetings which he did regularly. He bought East Mount, also known as Paradise House, and donated it to Scarborough Corporation in 1918. It later became known as the Graham Sea Training School and its stables across the road were converted into workshops. When the school bought a schooner to use as a training ship in 1925, they re-named it 'The Maisie Graham'; it was replaced in 1935 but kept the same name. North Riding County Council took over responsibility for all state education in 1944, then, with the arrival of comprehensive education in 1973, the old Boys' High School on Woodlands Drive became the Graham School with a Sea Training section to cater for pupils interested in a career at sea.

It is interesting to note that Paradise House has been part of Scarborough's history across the centuries. From its beginnings as the probable home of the Cistercian monks in the 12th century, it later became the home of the shipbuilding Tindall family, birthplace of Sir George Cayley and school for training many of the town's seafarers. Converted into residential flats, it gives the most wonderful views across the South Bay as it stands proudly above the harbour in the second millennium.

Distribution of funds in 1921 and 1922 and some consequences

Randomly amongst the archives are lists of grants awarded by the SUSF in 1921 and 1922. They give an insight into how the system worked, the opportunities that were available to Scarborough pupils and the progress they made.

In 1921 three students each received a £60 Exhibition for Leeds University; they were Hilda Luccock, Herbert Martin and John Bernard Clapp. Nora Tetley received £15 to attend Birmingham Training College while R H Mitchell's grant was £25 for her Chemistry Studies at Westminster College. For their Music Studies Eric William Fenby received £13, and William Hewitt £50. The pupils awarded exhibitions to the Secondary Schools are not named but twelve scholars were each awarded £7 10s to attend St Martin's Grammar School; one full time student at the School of Art received £6 6s while nine other students received £2 2s each.

We are told that George Fowler from Central Council School was appointed to the vacant Scholarship at the School of Art in October 1921 in place of Muriel Watson who had been awarded a North Riding Exhibition. A sum of £25 4s was given to Mr Bevan as clothing and maintenance grants for pupils attending the Municipal School. £13 in maintenance grants was given to Mr Colclough for two scholars at the Sea Scouts School. Special maintenance grants of £5 each were given to George Clubley and William Elliott while A W Davies received a £4. 5s 6d clothing grant.

In January 1922 we find that a student at the School of Art had been offered a Scholarship at the Municipal School under Scarborough Education Committee, we are not told if it was for the full time scholar from 1921. George Dixon received a free place at the Municipal School and clothing grants were made to Lucy Astel, Walter Smith and Elizabeth Birkbeck. Five candidates were entered for the University Examination.

By July Hilda Luccock had gained a second class Honours English Degree; in 1925 Miss Luccock was appointed to Falsgrave Mixed Council School. Scarborough benefitted from the investment; she was teaching at St Martin's Primary School in the 1960s and retired while John was in his first teaching post there. Miss Tetley was awarded her grant of £15 for a third year; both Leslie Alvey and

Harold Wharton were given clothing grants. Although Annie Winifred Mary Harland and Irene Gordon Wray had been awarded University Exhibitions in August, we read that in September:

'having obtained a North Riding Senior Exhibition, the awards fell through'

The balance on Ernest Horsley's loan was ordered to be written off.

In October Oswald Henry Harland made a further payment of £10 on his loan and a further maintenance grant of 5s per week was awarded to Leslie Alvey. A loan for £50, interest free for three years, was given to Mr T Hunter; this was to pay the premium required to place his son as apprentice with Cayzer Irvine and Co Ltd, of the Clan Line Steamers Ltd. Instructions were given to the Clerk of the SUSF to pay this amount to the Shipping Company after the Articles of Apprenticeship had been produced.

An ongoing saga of one Herbert Martin, who was advanced a loan of £60, runs through the 1928 – 2000 Minute Book. In the 1911 Census we find 9 year old Herbert living at 5 Palace Hill with his father, an engineer, his mother and his grandmother. There are three older brothers still at home, one is a fisherman, another is a warehouseman, the other is still at school, plus his older sister. Herbert's loan for his third year at Leeds University took until 1942 to be paid off. No mention of it is made until the meeting of 10 April 1934 when we read:

'The loan to Herbert Martin not having been paid the Clerk was directed to write to him and inform him that the whole case would be laid before the Education Committee by whom he was employed unless a suitable arrangement for payment was made.'

Mr Martin's reply was read to the Committee at the following meeting, 3 July, in which he promised to make a payment in July the next year. The Committee was having none of this, they directed the Clerk to write to let him know: *'the Governors are not inclined to wait until then as they consider he should make a payment each month'*

In spite of the letter having been sent on 11 July, a similar instruction was again given to the Clerk at the meeting on 18 September 1934. It would appear that the threat to lay the facts of the case before his employing authority had not been carried out.

We have a result: on 2 October, it was reported that Herbert Martin had repaid £5 off his loan of £180; we must assume he had been given loans of £60 in all three years at university. The Governors were to arrange to put the case on a business basis to repay the balance. On 13 April 1937, £10 from H Martin appears in a list of sums 'received on account of loans'. Mr Herbert Martin is mentioned again on 2 September 1940, one year into the Second World War; he had promised to repay the loan in monthly instalments of £2. Are we surprised to learn at the meeting on 15 November that nothing had been received? He did, however, promise to pay the arrears by 23 November. Yet another disappointment, as reported on 15 January 1941. The Clerk was instructed to issue a Writ if the balance was not paid within seven days.

Pitifully the minutes of 4 March tell the result of this letter:

'Mr Martin had replied pleading his wife's ill-health as the reason for his failure to keep his promises and had, on request, supported his explanation with a Doctor's Certificate and promised to commence monthly instalments on 26 April of £5.'

The Governors agreed in the circumstances to this concession but said they would take legal proceedings without further notice if the payment was not made. At the meeting on 9 September 1941, the Clerk was

> '*instructed to issue a High Court Writ against Mr Herbert Martin for £145 balance of his loan forthwith.*'

Two payments were made. On 9 September the Committee was left with a balance of £120 outstanding. A further Writ was to be issued on 23 December. The Minutes of 14 April 1942 read:

> '*The Clerk reported that judgement had been signed in the High Court against Mr Herbert Martin for £120 balance of loan and for costs but that no payment has subsequently been received from him.*
> *Resolved that the Clerk be instructed to issue execution on the judgement preferably by attachment of Mr Martin's salary*'

Finally on 18 August 1942 the matter is resolved:

> '*arising from an enquiry to the Director of Education for Huddersfield preparatory to the issue of execution on the judgement against Herbert Martin an arrangement had been made whereby £3 a month is deducted by the Director of Education, Huddersfield, from Martin's salary and remitted to the Clerk by way of repayment of the judgement debt.*'

We cannot make a judgement on Mr Martin's reluctance to repay the loan or on what might appear to be draconian measures taken by the SUSF Governors to retrieve the money. In their defence we know that it was vital to the running of the charity that loans be repaid. As the minutes of 4 March 1941 record:

> *'it was resolved with reluctance that no new grants or loans should be made for training at Universities or Training Colleges this year apart from the Exhibition, owing to there being no funds available.'*

The committee managed to keep funding the maintenance grants for secondary education and those already at college and university but the six applicants in 1941 were turned down. The previous year Betty Moore, Dena Hebditch, and Joan Illingworth had applied for loans to attend Training College, Joan's had been the only one granted.

It is interesting to note the names of the governors on the Committee during the war years. They include Mr G W Boothby as the Chairman; Canon C Patteson of St Mary's Church; Revd P R Watts of St Thomas' Church; Mrs A A Daws JP; Aldermen J W Butler, GKG Pindar and E Smith; J W Estill; S Boyes; J S Rawling; R Underwood and H V Willings. No record is given of the bodies they represented but S Boyes was from the Forty Club, Mr Estill was an NUT member, Mr Underwood had followed William Ascough as Secretary to the Scarborough Education Committee and Mr Willings was his successor. In February 1940 condolences were sent to the family of Mr H E Donner who had been Clerk to the SUSF for over 45 years, Sydney McCloy took on the post. At the April meeting appreciation of Mr F A Tugwell's 36 years' of service of were recorded.

On a happier note, we learn of William Hewitt's success, he passed his examination for Associate of the Royal College of Organists; he too had been given a grant in 1921. We learn from the 1911 census that he was born in 1898, his father was a tin plate worker and whitesmith who had moved from Newborough to Moorland Road. It has been suggested on the Wells of Yorkshire website that he taught Eric Fenby. William Wells Hewitt studied under Dr George Bennett at Lincoln Cathedral having served in the Royal Air Force during the First World War. He became assistant organist at the Cathedral from 1922 to 1926 before taking the post as organist at Holy Trinity Church in Stratford-upon-Avon. In 1933 he moved to Canada where he was the organist at St James' Cathedral in Toronto until 1956. From 1940 to 1942 he was also Chairman of the Toronto Centre of the Royal College of Organists.

More recent donations

Miss Hilda Briggs, the last headmistress of the Girls' High School, moved to what had been the Boys' High School in Woodlands Drive in 1973, as head of Graham School, a mixed comprehensive. Scarborough Sixth Form College took over the Girls' High School premises in Sandybed Lane. Miss Briggs retired in 1978 and worked as a volunteer for many organisations. She had been a member of the Amicable Society since arriving in Scarborough in 1964 and began her service as one of the representatives on the SUSF committee the following year; she attended her last meeting on 23 January 2009.

To celebrate her 80th birthday, this intrepid lady who had travelled all round the world, abseiled down the side of the Grand Hotel. At 85 she parachuted from a plane to raise money for Age Concern and for her 90th birthday, Miss Briggs was planning a sleep-over in South Cliff Methodist Church to raise money for the Rainbow Centre. Sadly she died in May 2009 just a few weeks before the event; in her will she left £500 to the SUSF.

A bequest of £2,000 was received from Dr Dorothy Anderson of Stratford on Avon on 23 Sept 2011. When the Scarborough Forum of the Duke of Edinburgh Awards closed, a sum of £1,000 was donated to SUSF in June 2013.

Changes

Very few alterations were needed to the constitution of the Foundation. The 1944 Education Act made secondary education free to all, it took a while to implement and the

SUSF Committee considered the matter on 24 August 1945. They resolved to continue to watch the workings of the new act for twelve months. A meeting with the Secretary of North Yorkshire County Council Education Committee was requested but never materialised. The committee was already on the case before comprehensive education was set up in Scarborough and the school leaving age was raised to 16 years in 1972.

Up to this time the Amicable Society took responsibility for children in need under the age of 15, SUSF worked with the older children and covered students attending universities or institutions of higher education. Alderman Miles Bird was elected Chairman that year and Councillor Clifford Morley was the Clerk. The committee included Councillor Bob Bedford, Mrs M F Kennedy, Miss Hilda Briggs, Mrs M L Priestley, Mr E Moor, Mr Maurice Horspool, Mr H Wilkinson, Revd J Keys Fraser, County Councillor Ralph Kenway Rowntree, Miss J Sinclair and Mr Don Harrison, the Divisional Education Officer.

A more significant change came, however, on 18 September 1987 when Canon J Keys Fraser brought to the notice of the meeting that the Governors of the John Kendall Trust, of which he was Chairman, were seeking the permission of the Charity Commission either to wind up the Trust or to transfer their assets to the SUSF. Of the people attending the meeting, Canon Fraser and Councillor H R Bedford were members of both Charities, incidentally Mr Bedford was also a member of the Amicable Society as was Miss Briggs.

A year later at their meeting in the Town Hall it was resolved that the Trustees of the Scarborough United Scholarships Foundation would also be the Trustees of the John Kendall Trust and that in future the John Kendall Trust meeting would be followed immediately by the meeting of the Scarborough United Scholarships Foundation. This had been the decision of the Charity Commission with the condition that the two charities be run entirely separately.

The Charity Commission made a concession in June 2005 when a request for a Uniting Direction was granted: both charities could be run in the same meeting, thus avoiding two similar sets of minutes, although the accounts must be kept separately.

*

PART FIVE
The Scarborough Amicable Society

Robert North

Robert North

> 'This Institution (originated by Robert North, Esquire) was founded 26 March, 1729, for the purpose of Clothing and Educating the Children of the Poor of Scarborough.'

This sentence prefaces almost every report written about the Amicable Society, often with the addition,

> 'It is Scarborough's oldest children's charity and possibly the oldest in the country.'

Who then was this Robert North? Revd John North became Vicar of St Mary's Church in 1696 while Revd Henry Docker was master of the Grammar School. John North had local connections as he was born in 1673 to Robert North, gentleman, from Ayton and Ann, née Saunders, from Scarborough. John had been educated at the Grammar School in Coxwold before going to Magdalene College in 1688. Six years after his arrival in the Parish, their only child, Robert, was born in the Vicarage, which at that time was in Queen Street. His baptism at St Mary's Church is recorded as 2nd November 1702. Sadly his father died in 1708 and Robert was brought up in an all-female household. Henry Docker took over as Vicar when John North died.

In his *'Scarborough Repository and Mirror of the Season, Volume 1'* published in 1824, John Cole wrote an article about the late Robert North, Founder of the Amicable Society. His information on Robert's education is vague, he simply says,

> 'after completing his studies at one of the universities he visited the continent and was distinguished for the refinement of his taste and manners'.

John Venn's Alumni Cantabrigienses tells us that Robert went to Mr Peacock's school in Wakefield before going to Christ College, Cambridge where he matriculated in 1720. In later life he became something of a recluse only venturing out of doors to go to church on Sundays. However, once every year he used his early experiences to good effect to entertain his female friends:

> *'whom he charmed by his polite attention, the brilliancy of his wit, the anecdotes of his travels, and a variety of interesting observations.'*

The rest of the year he spent alone. It is said he eccentrically walked about the streets making *'ejaculatory prayers or fervent aspirations'* and was convinced he would see the millennium.

Although John Cole and the writer of the first available Amicable Society Minute Book give the date of its inception as 1728, everywhere else it is given as 26th March 1729. Thomas Hinderwell explained the founder's motivation for setting up Scarborough Amicable Society when he gave an address on the revision of the Rules in 1804. Robert had been

> *'moved with sympathy at the destitute situation of the Children of the Poor, who were cast upon the wide wilderness of the world unprotected and untutored'.*

Robert North persuaded his friends and the good people of the town to subscribe 3d a week to the society to educate these children which, with the proceeds of special Church Services, proved sufficient to keep the Society going. They catered for the boys first, a master and twenty scholars attended school in a room at the Trinity House; eight years later they opened a department for ten girls.

The earliest minute book we have was started on 14 May 1835, coincidental with the 1835 Municipal Corporations Reform Act. In beautiful copperplate, the writer tells us that in 1728, when Mr Robert North was the first President

> *'there were 91 members and Twenty Boys were admitted upon the Institution'*

Although Robert North himself did not see the millennium, he was buried on 14 October 1760, the Amicable Society he created continues well beyond 2000.

Thomas Hinderwell, seafarer, collector of fossils and author of 'History of Scarborough' first published in 1798, was very active in the early years of the Amicable Society. He was born in 1744, also educated at Coxwold Grammar School and became President of the Society in 1784. He had known Robert North but possibly did not agree with him on all matters; he was the Chairman of the Committee of Revision and in his address, written on 23 January 1804, he described the times as 'alarming' and 'of extreme depravity'.

'the prevalence of licentiousness and infidelity endangers the existence of every civil and religious establishment...'

He further explains:

'the appellation of the AMICABLE SOCIETY. This appropriate title was chosen, to indicate the blessings and advantages, which flow from a cordial union, and to be a perpetual MEMENTO, to induce members to connect themselves in bonds of indissoluble harmony...

It would be commendable to transmit the Institution, in an improved state, to posterity ... and that the AMICABLE SOCIETY will continue to dispense its blessings through the revolution of ages.'

Not only did the Amicable Society teach children the rudiments of education whilst caring for their wellbeing, they also provided each child with an apprenticeship on leaving school together with a Bible, a Prayer Book and a copy of Hinderwell's 'Admonitions' also written in 1804. Mr

Thomas Hinderwell appears in the list of Principal Benefactions, donating £50 in 1825.

The First Amicable Schools

The original benefactions are well documented both in the hand written ledgers and in the Annual Reports. The first is Mr Fish (also written 'Fysh') no date is given:

> *Tristram Fish, Esq., erected the late West Gallery in the Church, for the use of the children.*
>
> *1791 The Rev. Barnard Foord, LLD., assigned two annual rents or payments of Ten Shillings each, issuing out of certain premises situate near St. Nicholas Cliff, in front of the houses Nos. 7b and 9.*
>
> *1793 Mr. George Fowler bequeathed Fifty Pounds.*
>
> *1794 Mr. John Ward, the field called Cockhill Close, Ramshill.*
>
> *1817 Mr Thomas Hewitson, Five Hundred Pounds*

A marble plaque was erected in St Mary's Church to commemorate John Ward's benevolence. It read:

> *THIS MARBLE ERECTED to perpetuate the Remembrance of the Exemplary Beneficence of JOHN WARD, GENT: who impressed with the desire to alleviate the miseries of poverty and to inculcate the principle of Religion and Industry generously bequeathed Six Hundred Pounds to an Institution for clothing and educating the children of the Poor of Scarborough under the patronage of the Amicable Society,*
>
> *28 July, 1794.'*
>
> *Charity hopeth all things.*

When Mr A Rowley, the Church Warden, contacted the Trustees with a view to reinstating the plaque which had fallen from the wall, the minutes of 13 November 1936 reveal that the plaque was beyond repair.

Over the years many more names were added to the list of benefactors, their contributions paid for the provision of the school as well as the education of the boys and girls. From the later Annual Reports we learn:

'Out of the foregoing Benefactions, the old School-rooms with residences for the Master and Mistress, were built in 1817, at the expense of upwards of £1,200, on ground given by the Corporation of Scarborough.'

This was a single storey building on the corner of what is now Castle Road and Auborough Street but was then known as Duesbury (Dewsbery) Walk.

The original Amicable School

The earliest Minute Book is a large calf bound tome with gold stippling and an embossed title 'AMICABLE SOCIETY BYE LAW BOOK 1835' on the front. Thanks to the fastidiousness of the writer we have a list of the great and the good of Scarborough who subscribed to the charity. The three earliest names are Miss Dowker of Salton, Miss Robson and Miss Burton of London. Donations were received from Mr A Beswick in 1781, then Miss Taylor and Mrs Kirk a year later.

    1794 was a good year, John Woodall Esq., Dr Travis and His Grace the Duke of Rutland all became members on 20 January. In 1800 they were joined by Edward Donner, other Scarborough family names include John Tindall, Mr William B Fowler, Mr William Bean, W J Denison Esq. London (the family name of the Londesboroughs), Mr Henry Fowler (who declined in arrears in 1835) Mr S S Byron who declined in 1836, Sir J V B Johnstone, Bart in 1824 and two years later Sir Thomas Legard, Bart. Mr William Palliser appears on 16 April 1827 and later that year John Woodall (Jun) joins them. We keep meeting up with many of these characters throughout this book, they were the 'movers and shakers' of their time.

    It is no coincidence that on 17 December 1832 Col. Sir Frederick Trench KCH appears next to Sir George Cayley, Sir Frederick had just succeeded Sir George as Conservative MP for Scarborough in the days when Scarborough returned two MPs. It notes that John Woodall died in 1835. These lists of members are also repeated in the Annual Reports together with the addresses and the amount paid; half a guinea entitled each member to a vote while a whole guinea gave two votes. The normal subscription was 3d per week, usually paid as 13 shillings a year. Collecting boxes were placed in churches, businesses and public houses and the wardens were responsible for them.

    By the time Will Palliser became President in 1835, the Amicable Society had existed for more than a century. He was a farrier living at 21 Huntriss Row, in 1841 he and his wife Jane had six children; his immaculate signature graces the Minutes which he may also have written. Among the meticulous records we find a table of members and another of boys and girls. From them we discover that in 1740, 89 members supported 26 boys and 10 girls; by 1820, 299 members helped 50 boys and 22 girls. The first three boys listed in the book are Benjamin Normandale, John Cowlam and William Dalton, all admitted in 1830. The girls were Elizabeth Hogg, admitted in 1828, Catherine Normandale and Harriet Garbutt who came in 1830.

We also learn that in 1835, together with Mr Palliser, the Trustees were W B Fowler, a ship owner living in Princess Street, Zachariah T Wellburn, who had a grocer's shop in Newborough Street, Henry Woodall who lived with his brother in St Nicholas House and Thomas Smurthwaite who was the Manager of the Savings Bank in King Street.
The four Wardens were William Sedman, a butcher with premises in Leading Post Street; James Dale, an Iron Monger in Newborough Street; Mark Ruddock, Innkeeper at the Blacksmith's Arms in Queen Street and Solomon Wilkinson Theakston. Mr Theakston had a book shop at 31 St Nicholas Street where he was the proprietor of the Scarborough Gazette employing 11 men and 6 boys. His 'Guide to Scarborough' originally published in 1864 gives a contemporary insight into life in Scarborough.

Funds were raised at St Mary's Church from collections during the year, some being in 'the season' when invited preachers gave a sermon. John Cole recounts that on 8 August 1824, Revd S Wass, standing in for the Vicar, preached on Matthew XVIII 14, *'it is not the will of your Father that one of these little ones should perish.'* The congregation duly 'opened wide their hands' and £25.12s was added to the Amicable Society's coffers.

The four sermons in 1835 raised a total of £67.6s.4½d. Whether these preachers happened to be on holiday in the town or whether they came specially we are not told but Revd C H Lutwidge, Vicar of Burton Agnes raised £21.3s.9d, Revd Charles Hodgson, Rector of Barton le Street raised £18.6s.5d, Revd I R Inge of Trinity College, Cambridge brought in £15.2s.5d while Revd Miles Jackson, Minister of St Paul's in Leeds managed £12.13s.9½d. Eight gentlemen were appointed as Collectors for St Mary's Church and a further eight for Christ Church. The membership of the Society totalled 293 with 45 boys and 25 girls to support. 1835 was Mr J Mitchell's last year as headmaster, his salary was £60 and the mistress, Mrs Ann Marshall, had a salary of £25.

'On entering the school the boys received a suit, cap, trousers, waistcoat, two shirts, a pair of boots and two pairs of stockings. The girls were given a cloak, a dress, hat, an apron, two pairs of stockings and a pair of boots, with supplementary issues at Christmas.'

We are given exact details of the cost of providing the complete uniform for all the pupils and the names of the suppliers. Shoes at 3/10 (3 shillings and ten pence) a pair were supplied by J Simpson; J Armstrong made the boys' clothing at 5/- per suit, J Leasley furnished the cloth at 3/- per yard, the Worsted came from Thomas Law at 3/1 a yard for the brown and 3/3 a yard for the blue. The boys wore swallow tail coats and knee breeches, topped with a skull cap while the girls were attired in gowns of brown serge, a bonnet and white cotton mittens, they wore long cloaks in cold weather. Each child had a second set of clothes to wear on Sundays, these were kept in a canvas bag which was handed out on Fridays and returned to school on Mondays.

The first record in this book is of a special meeting held at The London Inn on 14 May 1835 where it was agreed to alter the shape of the boys' caps. In June that year, John Woodall Esq., Town Clerk, was thanked for the *'handsome gift of the organ in the Girls School room'* at a meeting in the Spread Eagle Inn. The meeting in July was held in the Boys' School Room when the committee discussed the pupils' examinations; they would include Crossman's Introduction to the Christian Religion, 24th Chapter of St Luke's Gospel, 1st and 2nd Chapters of the Acts of the Apostles, with spelling from these chapters, Cyphering and their Copy Books would be exhibited.

In October at their meeting in The Old King's Arms, the trustees decided to purchase just one copy of a book on Psalmody, 'for the use and practice of the Children belonging to the Society', which was about to be published by Mr W Wilson. The meeting on 5 November in the Spread Eagle Inn became heated when it was carried that three boys, Thomas Clark, Thomas Claybourne and William Ford, be brought before the Bailiffs *'for continually annoying and insulting the Master and Children of the Society.'* On 21 December in the Elephant and Castle Inn, a committee was drawn up to appoint a Master for the Boys' School following the resignation of Mr Mitchell, he had found a better position in Long Preston in the West Riding.

At the Committee Meeting in the Boys' School on 28 December they agreed to instruct Revd M H Miller

> *'to write to the Secretary of the National Society London to request him to find a competent person to fill the duties of Teacher of the Boys' School.'*

As a consequence, Septimus Schollick, *'a widower and turned of 40'*, native of Ulverston and *'much superior to Mr Mitchell'*, was appointed to start in the following June on a salary of £60 with free accommodation. Mr Schollick, with a competent knowledge of English Grammar was also able to offer Arithmetic, Mensuration, Book Keeping, Navigation, Algebra and Geometry. He remained Head of the school until 1860 when he retired on a pension of half his salary.

Boys from the Amicable School around 1860

We find a copy of an abject letter of apology, penned by Thomas Smurthwaite on 8 February 1836 when the committee again met at the London Inn. It was reported to the next meeting at Mrs Croft's Star Inn and sent to the

Mayor. The problem? Mr Palliser had inadvertently omitted to *'distinguish Mr Byron by the title of Mayor'* in its list of Members of the Society for the past year. They were sorry that the matter could not be remedied as it would incur vast expense to rewrite the list in a new book.

So we discover that the transition from Common Hall to Borough Council, housed in the Assembly Rooms in St Nicholas Street, was an important issue in 1835. It was particularly important to its first Mayor one S S Byron Esq. aged 35, Magistrate from Hutton Buscel. We met him conducting the trial in the Bleach House case two years earlier when John Woodall, Edward Donner, William Thornton and Henry Fowler had been accused of misappropriating £35 at the election. As well as being of the 'old order', these burgesses were subscribers to the Amicable Society, as was Mr Byron until 1836.

Celebrations in 1860

On 14 May 1860 a new headmaster was appointed due to the imminent retirement of Mr Schollick at Midsummer. The meeting took place in the Castle Hotel, Queen Street with Mr Richard Mosey in the Chair. The successful candidate, Mr Moses Archer of 32 Blenheim Terrace, Scarborough, was elected. Whether or not it was to commemorate Mr Schollick's 24 years as headmaster, the Celebration Day on 28 July 1860 seems to have been a particularly joyful occasion as recorded in the minutes by Councillor Dr W H Rooke.

Celebration Day was originally designed as a festive picnic in Cockhill Close, the field donated by John Ward in 1794. The pupils gathered at the school then marched with silken banners behind a drum and fife band. They crossed the Cliff Bridge:

> *'by kind permission of the Directors and went to the New Music Saloon where they sang 'Rule Britannia'*

and God Save the Queen with remarkable effect and received a good round of applause from the company assembled. Arriving at the close they each received 6d., and were regaled with bread and cheese being in accordance with the will of the donor of the field.'

John Ward's Oration was read before the picnic which was followed by games. A copy of the Oration can be found in the Cock Hill Close Trust section. On the return journey they called at St Mary's Vicarage, which was in The Crescent, to sing *'appropriate tunes and cheered the Vicar heartily.'* The Vicar in 1860 was Revd John William Whiteside. Dr Rooke noted that they had been
'favoured with the unusual luxury of a marching-day without rain.'

In addition to the picnic, at six o'clock that year, thanks to the President, Richard Mosey Esq. and Dr Rooke, the children were taken to visit *'the menagerie exhibiting in Scarborough'* where they were *'highly entertained and instructed.'*
    There is no doubt that the Anniversary Dinner held at Mr Brown's Millers Hotel on 2 January 1861 was to honour Septimus Schollick. After a sumptuous dinner which was enjoyed by 53 members, Revd Dr Whiteside, the Vicar, presented him with a 'Handsome Time Piece' and a purse, subscribed voluntarily by the members of the Institution.

A New School for the Amicable Society

A year later, the secretary at the Annual Meeting on 8 January 1862, again held in Mr Wilkcs Brown's Millers Hotel was very thorough. Mr R H Peacock presided over the business which *'was conducted according to the accustomed routine.'* John Haigh sen. was elected President; the trustees were Mr Charles Hill, Mr Edward Dove, Mr Wiliam Hart and Mr George Welburn while the Wardens elected were Mr

William Stewart, Mr William Stansfield, Mr William Drury and Mr John Stephenson.

The Ladies Committee consisted of Miss C A Woodall (Caroline Althea, daughter of William the solicitor), Miss Uppleby, Miss E Woodall (Edith, daughter of John the Magistrate, cousin to Caroline) Miss Weddell, Miss Hebden (Elizabeth) and Miss E Tate. On the Examination Committee were Mr John Hebden, Dr W F Rooke, Mr John Beckett, Mr S Bailey, Mr Richard Mosey and Mr George Porrett. To complete the picture we have the Musical Committee with Captain J W Woodall (Edith's brother), Mr J Leckenby, Mr S Bailey, Mr W Woodall (Solicitor, father of Caroline), Mr W Hebden (brother to Elizabeth and banker with John Woodall), Mr R H Peacock and Mr Smallwood.

The next meeting on 17 January was convened to receive tenders for clothing etc. This time suits, cord trousers, calico and cloth for girls' cloaks went to Mr William Rowntree, shoes and repairs to Mr William Coates, Mr Thomas Mackwood was to provide serge, worsted and flannel while Mr William Adamson had the tender for bonnets and Mr William Wright was to supply check, linen and 'smallwares'. Stationary went to Mr George Crosby, ironmongery to Mr Paul Lord, Mr Henry Hornsey was appointed plumber and glazier, Mr Stockdale painting. Mr R C Cass supplied the brushes and grocery. We now have a bricklayer, Mr Benjamin Smith; a joiner, Mr J Kelby and finally a 'haircutter', Mr Benjamin Holmes.

Perhaps Mr Archer found his accommodation unsuitable for within a short time the Committee was appointing collectors to canvas for subscriptions towards the School Building fund in order to replace the original school. We are told:

In 1863 these buildings were pulled down; new and commodious Schoolrooms, with residences for the teachers, being erected in their stead: partly by special subscriptions, and partly from funds belonging to the Institution.

This building was of Gothic design, brick built with blue and green slates, the rooms were each 20 feet by 15 feet, designed to accommodate 200 pupils, well lit and warmed by open fireplaces. Additional subscriptions had been sought to help pay for the new building. The school closed in 1893 and the building was later converted into houses that are still recognisable as part of the original school on Castle Road, the playground forms the car park in front of 'The Scarborough Arms'.

Rules and Regulations

A set of rules was drawn up in 1866 when Richard Cross, Esq. was President; Revd R F L Blunt headed the Committee of Revision two years after replacing Dr Whiteside as Vicar of Scarborough. Also on the committee were John Woodall, Esq.; A Gibson Esq., Mayor; W E Woodall Esq.; J P Moody, Esq.; J Haigh, Esq. and S Bailey, Esq. It explains in detail how the Trustees and Wardens should be elected, what their duties were, what clothes the children should be given and that each child would be *'furnished with a bible and a common prayer book'*. The means of selecting the children was:

'When a vacancy shall happen in either of the schools, the President shall cause public notice thereof to be given by the Bellman, and a written or printed notice containing the names of the candidates, together with the names and occupation, &c., of their parents, shall be sent to each Member on or before the Election, so that the Members may be enabled to judge of their eligibility.

> *Illegitimate children, and all others who are under eight years of age or above eleven, shall be inadmissible; and no person shall be permitted to have more than two children on the Institution at the same time.*

The 28th July Procession and the 'treat in remembrance of the late Mr Thomas Huitson' on 6th September were both written into the rules. The cover to this booklet also mentions

'ADMONITIONS GIVEN TO EACH CHILD ON LEAVING THE INSTITUTION'

William Tindall received such a book on 4 November 1878, it was printed by J Grice, Printer of Newborough Street and gives instructions as to how the children should behave after leaving school: they should remember the kindness the Society has shown them, keep their faith, be loyal to their masters and avoid drunkenness and gaming. A copy of another uplifting book, *'Old Transome'*, was also given to William the year before. It was written by Hesba Stretton, a Methodist evangelical writer of children's books, it is a somewhat sentimental Victorian tale of overcoming poverty by scholarship and faith. Both these books are in the tin trunk.

Annual Reports of the Amicable Society's Schools were produced in booklet form. The earliest one in the archives is for 1879 to 1880, printed by T Taylor and Son, "Railway Guide" Offices, Newborough, when Henry Cross was the Secretary and Charles W Woodall the President. Later Reports were printed by ETW Dennis, Printer and Bookseller, 82 Newborough and others by Geo. Pindar of 45 St Thomas Street. Up to the start of the First World War, each report contained the names of the Officers, a list of the Members, the date they began to subscribe and their address, details from the accounts, a list of the 'Principal Benefactions – The Appropriation Thereof' (giving the amount donated), a 'Statement of the Instruction Given' and the 'Progress of the Society' i.e. the number of members each year together with the number of boys and girls educated.

In the year from Sept. 30th 1883, to Sept. 30th, 1884 Mr William Peacock was the President with Mr G S Wellburn, Mr H M Cross, Mr E T W Dennis and Mr G D Smith Jun. as Trustees. The Wardens were Mr J H Smethurst, Mr R Smith, Mr S W Fisher and Mr J Hagyard; the Treasurer was William Hebden Esq. and the Bankers were Messes. Woodall, Hebden & Co. Miss Hebden sat on the Ladies Committee with Miss Tate, Mrs J W Taylor, Mrs E H Newton, Miss Nesfield, Miss A Tindall, Miss Broomhead and Miss A Hick. The Honorary Secretary was none other than Mr William Ascough, he had taken on the post in 1880, the year after his arrival as Clerk to the Scarborough School Board. Mr J Beckwith was the Auditor and the Teachers were Mr Josiah Wilson and Miss Pateman.

Even in these days the schools had the equivalent of OFSTED in their 'Report to the President, Wardens, and Members of the Amicable Society', theirs was 'payment by results'. HMI T S Aldis had examined the schools and as a result of this inspection the total Government Grant awarded was £78. 16s. 9d, which was £5 more than in the previous year. Of the forty-four boys, 42 had passed in reading, 41 in writing and 40 in arithmetic, they also passed in grammar, geography and 'singing from notes', five passed in algebra and three in navigation. Out of the forty-one girls, 37 passed in reading, 30 in writing but only 26 in arithmetic, with the addition of singing and needlework. Ten girls had obtained the grant for practical cookery. The Ladies Committee, separate from the main committee, had decided:

'the girls should continue the instruction in cookery... It is felt that the knowledge gained will be beneficial to the girls completing their time at school in after life, either as servants, or in their own homes.'

The last page announces that the Society's Anniversary is celebrated on the First Wednesday after New Year's Day. 'Ordinary Meetings' are held on the first Monday in every month 'at Seven o'clock p.m.' in the Girls' Schoolroom. Perhaps the part that would cause the most excitement is the final paragraph:

> 'On the 28th July and 6th September, the respective birthdays of the late Mr John Ward, and Mr. Thomas Hewitson, liberal benefactors to this Institution, as specified in the list of Bequests, the children go in procession to receive sixpence each, at the place appointed by the Testator.'

Thanks to Frank Green, Secretary of the Amicable Society from 1974 to 1984, we have it on good authority that for the celebration on 6 September each year, the birthday of one Thomas Hinston (or Hewitson as he appears in the list of principal benefactions) each pupil received a sixpenny piece and an orange. He instanced a past pupil he had known who thought this was his own birthday as it was the only time he received a present, thus showing the poverty of many Amicable children.

The Society's Anniversary continued to take the form of a Christmas Dinner with roast beef and plum pudding served in one of the town's hostelries, often The Bull Inn, after the children had marched along Castle Road to attended divine service in the morning. The children were accompanied by the teachers and several officers and other friends of the Society then the President joined them and would give out gifts for the children.

In the evening a 'party of gentlemen' would also have a meal when many toasts were made; to the Queen, to the Archbishop of York and the clergy of various denominations, to the Amicable Society and to the health of the Member of Parliament. The Secretary then gave the Annual Report before a toast was made to the President, this was followed by a toast to the Mayor, another to the Wardens and Trustees and finally to the Ladies, who were not present.

The Cock Hill Close Trust

Cock Hill Close (also written Cockhill) was the field donated to the Amicable Society by John Ward in 1794, off Ramshill and is now occupied by Royal Crescent. The Cockhill Close Investment had a separate set of trustees; in 1794 eleven had been appointed, it was renewed in 1829 when only three members were left. and yet again on 11 December 1854.

In 1842, at the behest of Revd M H Miller, Vicar of St Mary's, J H Coulson, Dr Travis and Mr Thomas Hart, it was resolved that Mr W B Coulson, Solicitor *'be asked to serve the necessary notices for Mr Hudson to quit Cock Hill Close'* in favour of a member of the Society. Mr W B Coulson was the Registrar of the Court of Pleas.

On 11 December 1854 John Woodall, Esq.; Harcourt Johnstone Esq.; W Woodall, Esq.; Mr J Cook; Mr J Uppleby, Town Clerk; Mr E J Nesfield; Mr William Hebden and Mr William Laycock were elected Trustees of Cockhill Close at Blanchard's Hotel on Huntriss Row. The President of the Amicable Society at the time was Revd Dr John William Whiteside, Vicar of St Mary's Church; the Treasurers had been elected in January 1851, they were bankers, Messrs Woodall, Hebden and Hardcastle. In 1880 the Cockhill Close Trustees had dropped from eight to five, they were E H Hebden, Esq., Sir H Johnstone, Bart., John Woodall, Esq., W E Woodall, Esq. and Wm Hebden, Esq.

Sir Harcourt Johnstone was one of Scarborough's two MPs from 1869 until 1880 when he was made a Peer as Lord Derwent of Hackness. E H Hebden and his brother William were the sons of Edward H Hebden, Banker. William went into the business and lived at Throxenby Hall while E H remained in the family home, 6 Belvoir Terrace with his sister Elizabeth. He was registered 'deaf and dumb from birth' on the census forms and his occupation appears as 'dividends'. Charles Woodall, President in 1880, was brother to Jonathan Woodall Woodall, sons of John Woodall, Banker, grandsons of John Woodall, Town Clerk, who died in 1835.

In the Amicable Society Report of 1880 we read that:

'The property at present belonging to the Institution, consists only of the schools above mentioned; £5,500 realised by the sale of Cockhill Close, and now invested in Three Per Cent. Consols, the interest of which brings in £172 6s 4d per annum'.

Only William Hebden and Lord Derwent are named as The Cockhill Close Trustees in 1881. The 1884 Annual Report of the Amicable Society reiterates the sale of Cockhill Close that realised £5,500 which was invested. It also mentions that 10s each came from the two annual rents on St. Nicholas Cliff which must have been those donated in 1791 by Revd Barnard Foord. There were fifty-five shares in the Cliff Bridge Company which had come from the investment of a hundred pounds contributed by His Grace the late Archbishop of York in 1827. When SUSF amalgamated with the Amicable Society in 1904, the Cockhill Close Charity was handed to them.

This is a copy of the oration read on Celebration Day. The original was written on vellum.

'ANNUALLY ON 28th OF JULY

Gentlemen and Friends to the Amicable Society,

We are now assembled to commemorate the liberality of Mr. John Ward, a generous Benefactor to this Institution, and that his generosity may be fully known both for the interests of the Charity and as a laudable example to others I am directed by the President of the Society to recite to you those clauses of the Will which relate to the Institution; and also to inform you what Measures have been adopted to give full effect to the charitable Intentions of the Donor.

The Clauses referred to are as follows:- "I give and bequeath unto John Woodall of Scarborough Esq., and Richard Smith Robson of Scarborough, Gentleman, and the Survivor of them and to the executors or administrators of such Survivor for ever, the sum of Six hundred pounds of lawful Money of Great Britain upon Trust, that they, the said John Woodall and Richard Smith Robson or the Survivor of them or the executors or administrators of such Survivor shall and do apply and appropriate the said sum of Six hundred pounds to and for the use and benefit of the Amicable Society in Scarborough, in such a manner as the said John Woodall and Richard Smith Robson or the Survivor of them shall think most proper and I do hereby charge and make liable my close or Parcel of Land called Cockhill Close containing about six acres with the Stable or Cowhouse and appurtenances thereto belonging purchased by my late Aunt, Elizabeth Nightingale, of Mr Peter Goullett situate near Ramsden and within the Liberties of Scarborough aforesaid and now occupied by John Temple to and with the payment of six hundred pounds accordingly.

And my intention is and I do hereby direct and desire that the Officers of the said Society and such other Members thereof, as shall think proper shall and do yearly and every year for ever upon the Twenty-eighth day of July about Noon being the day of my Birth assemble on or near the said Cockhill Close and that out of the Interest or Annual Produce of the said sum of Six hundred pounds there shall be distributed and paid to each Boy and Girl then upon the Institution of the said Society who must also attend the sum of Sixpence in remembrance of Me. And at the same time I order and direct that the Gentlemen who shall attend such Meeting shall also thereout be refreshed or regaled with Cake and Wine.

In order to render this Bequest beneficial and permanently secure the Trustees above named have executed an Assignment of Cockhill Close in trust to eleven Members of this Society (five of whom are now living) to appropriate the Rents and Profits of these premises to the purposes designed by the Will and with the provision that when the Number shall be reduced to three by Death or otherwise new trustees shall be elected by the Members of the said Society from time to time for the said Purposes for ever. These children the Objects of his and your generous care will now offer up their Annual Tribute of Praise and Thanksgiving to the Giver of all good Gifts and may his Providence continue to protect the Institution more and more to Succeeding Generations'.

Closure of the schools

School attendance in 1891 had dwindled to only 34 boys and 30 girls; the Elementary Instruction was described as *'fairly good'* but in order for the higher grant to be recommended, *'Grammar would have to improve considerably.'* The 'Celebration Day' treat had been a visit to Wykeham, courtesy of the President, the Revd J C Simpson. In this year James Henry Rowntree joined the committee; he was brother to William Stickney Rowntree and also worked in the drapers store in Westborough.

With the passing of the Elementary Education Act 1891 free elementary education was available to all children in the borough. The Annual Report records that a circular and voting paper had been sent to all 264 subscribers to the society with the result that:

'Only 19 votes were in favour of the continuance of the Charity in its present form'.

It is signed by W Ascough and H Chapman, Honorary Secretaries, and its final paragraph expresses the wishes of the Committee:

It is their earnest desire that this ancient Charity which has done great and noble work for the past 163 years, may by further development prove even a greater blessing and be of more extended usefulness in the future, if possible, than in the past.'

The circular points out that simply from the income derived from investments, without taking subscriptions into account, 76 children could have been clothed; the average attendance of children over the previous 6 years was 76. It was emphasised that they wished *'to make the Society something more than a clothing charity.'*

It was felt that children would have a more efficient education if they attended other Public Elementary Schools in the town; as Secretary to the School Board, William Ascough was able to speak with authority on this matter. The committee had decided that the establishment of an orphanage would be impracticable, they preferred to use the whole income for *'Clothing and fitting the children for after life.'* There would be sufficient *'to give outfits to girls on leaving school for service, and apprenticeship fees to enable boys on leaving to learn a trade; as well as continue Christmas dinners, treats and gifts of sixpences.'* The children would continue to be elected in the same way to *'benefit the deserving poor'.*

It was also hoped *'that the School buildings might be used in some beneficial way.'*

To satisfy the Charity Commissioners in 1892, a Special Committee sought legal advice to ensure the bequests and donations could be used this way. The decision was to be made at a meeting the following year.

For their treat Captain Darley, President, gave the children a train trip to Hayburn Wyke. The Annual Meeting ran on the usual lines, after the Church Service, a meal of roast beef and plum pudding was served at the Talbot Hotel. Captain Darley presented the gift of a timepiece to Miss Eden who was leaving to marry Mr Maurice Williams of Oswestry. Mr Ascough announced in his report that

> 'the schools would be discontinued after the examination by Her Majesty's Inspector in June next'.

Sir George Sitwell attended the dinner and proposed the toast to his successor as MP, Mr Joshua Rowntree,

> 'although he did not agree with him in politics yet he had the greatest esteem and liking for him as a fellow townsman.'

Responding, Mr Rowntree said he regretted that Sir George was leaving the town to return to Derbyshire:

> 'The one especial bond of union which bound them together, and in which no difference of opinion existed, was their common interest in the Amicable Society.'

Joshua Rowntree was Scarborough's MP from 1886 to 1892; he was both preceded and succeeded by Sir George Sitwell.

On 27 February 1893 a special general meeting was held at the Old Savings Bank in King Street where the future of the Society was discussed in great depth. It was eventually agreed that the school building could be leased but if a good offer was made, it could be sold. The parents would to be allowed to choose which Public Elementary School their child would attend. The argument divided along denominational lines as to whether the Church of England should be preferred, particularly as attendance at Sunday School was compulsory and the schools had always been connected to the Church of England. Mr Ascough calmed the waters by suggesting the choice lay with the parents but the January Anniversary would be held in the Parish Church or Chapel of Ease and would be followed with roast beef and plum pudding.

The Secretary at the School Board Offices, William Ascough, wrote to the Charity Commission suggesting that the sum of £1,000 had been offered by the Charity Organizations Society for the building. However, the Committee decided to offer it on lease to North Riding County Council as a centre for Technical Instruction with a nominal rental of £10 per annum. The Charity Organizations Society (COS) was given the task of making the children's garments with a guarantee that the work is done *'to the satisfaction and approval of the Ladies' Committee.'*

The schoolmaster, Mr Wilson was given notice to terminate his services with the addition of three months' salary in consideration of his faithful service. He was to be allowed free tenancy of the School House until the end of September and he continued to keep a record of the children in the Society's care. In July 1893 Mr Chapman purchased the organ for £25; an offer of £15 was also made for the furniture.

One of the final tasks concerned the *'question of the disposal of the portrait of Mr Robert North the founder of the Amicable Society.'* Mr Fisher, a member from 1880 and one time Warden and Trustee, promised to have it properly cleaned and renovated before it was put on loan to the School Board. Mrs Ruston was appointed as Caretaker and allowed the house free of rent. The portrait now hangs in the Committee Room at the Town Hall where the SUSF Committee currently meets.

Seeking a New Role

Although the Amicable Schools no longer existed, the newspaper reported that the Amicable Society had celebrated its Annual Dinner in 1894 with seventy of the eighty-four children, now dispersed in various schools, attending the service at Christ Church. It was followed by *'a capital dinner'* at the Bull Hotel. As the newly elected President, Mr John Dale JP, was in the place of honour on the top table at the Annual Dinner in the evening with the Mayor, Mr G L Beeforth JP, on his right and Captain Darley JP, the retiring President, on his left. Sir George Sitwell MP had sent his apologies.

The Revd C C Mackarness in responding to a toast asked where there was a gap in education now that free elementary education had arrived. He thought the Society should look to helping the children of the poor to reach university and they were proposing to offer a scholarship, something that had not previously been possible. Mr Darley's praises were sung as he had held office over a very anxious two years while great changes had been made. Mr Dale highlighted the plight of young boys leaving school at 14 and taking on employment as errand boys or boat boys. By the time they reached 18 there was no longer any work for them so they had no occupation, the Society would teach their boys a trade by which they would always be able to learn a living.

A presentation was made to Mr Ascough on behalf of the Amicable Society of a purse with an address inscribed on a *facsimile* of the Amicable Schools

To Mr. William Ascough.
Dear Sir, -- For some time it has been felt that the long and continuous services rendered to the Scarborough Amicable Society's schools should receive some recognition. The wise and necessary changes which have taken place so recently, to the

success of which you have contributed so materially, having been finally inaugurated, the present seems a most fitting time to mark our high appreciation for your interest in, and your services to, this old and valued society. We therefore wish to thank you for all you have done, and beg your acceptance of the purse and its contents which accompanies this testimonial, as a small token of our esteem and regard in which you are held. –We are, dear sir, on behalf of the subscribers,

Henry Darley (President)	*E. R. Roper,*
H. J. Morton,	*James H Rowntree,*
A. Atkinson	*Geo. Dale Smith,*
James Bland	*Henry Chapman*
Geo. T. Eaman	*T.F. Taylor (hon. sec)*

In his speech, Mr Morton, the instigator of the gift, gives an insight into William Ascough's character.

'Mr Ascough had been an intelligent and experienced guide even under very difficult circumstances. He had that gift which was very valuable... good judgement. He had found that even with awkward persons he somehow managed to put them in a fairly pleasant humour.'

Mr Ascough made a spontaneous reply saying that it would be sad if men were not willing to work for the good of the community without hope of any reward. He had been pleased to be asked to take charge of the secretarial matters and he was pleased to see the good and honest work the Society was doing. The purse, a small embroidered handbag, was the gift of Lilly Steble, wife of the past Mayor, Lt. Col. Richard Steble, to Mrs Ascough. It contained a cheque for £60.

The following year about a hundred children attended the Anniversary Service, held in the Parish Church in the morning; it was followed by *'an excellent dinner'* at the Talbot Hotel. At the Annual Meeting, held in the Savings Bank, King Street in the afternoon, it was noted that the Society had never before benefitted so many children. Mr John Dale was re-elected President and four wardens were elected, one of whom was Mr William Boyes of 8 Oak Road. He had become a member in 1885, four years after opening his small store on Eastborough. Interesting to note, Boyes Store, the family run business he started, continues to support the Society through gift tokens purchased at Christmas by the current Amicable Society.

That evening the Annual Dinner was held at the Talbot Hotel with the customary mix of gentlemen from differing professions, denominations and political persuasions. Reference was made to the opening of Scarborough Hospital, steered by Mr Dale in his capacity as Mayor, this hospital stood on Friars Way and is now a car park. William Ascough, emphasised that they subsisted on voluntary contributions and paid tribute to the tradesmen of Scarborough who had been the backbone of the society. He rounded off the speeches by referring to the *'compliment which the society had paid him last year at the time domestic afflictions were depressing him'* and to show his appreciation he had used £10 of the gift to pay for his life membership.

In addition to providing clothing for school outfits on leaving school and paying for training and apprenticeships, since 1893 the Society had also established scholarships from Elementary to Secondary Schools. William Ascough in his capacity as Clerk to the School Board had been instrumental in setting up the Scarborough United Scholarships Foundation in 1888. In the Annual Report of 1898, the committee noted their concern that, with the children spread across the town in the Day and Sunday Schools of their parents' choice, the officers rarely met the children to influence their characters for good. They suggested amending the rules so the children would attend an additional Sunday School each week to be held in the old school, this was to be organised by Mr Wilson, the late Headmaster.

The first session was planned for 3 July 1898 from 10 to 12 o'clock, a piano would be purchased, Mr Wilson would supply a syllabus of six months and he would be appointed Superintendent on a salary of £20, to include his present duties. However the minutes of 11 July state that as the rooms were not available, the Sunday School would be postponed until after the August holidays. The Sunday School began in October, the Officers attending in rotation, attendance was 'fairly satisfactory' and served as a valuable means of supervision as to the conduct, cleanliness and care of clothing.

In the Annual Report for 1898 mention is made that further help and direction should be given in 'special aid on leaving school'. A few months before leaving school the older girls would be properly instructed in housework, as a great proportion of girls enter domestic service.

'This would include: - firelaying, blackleading, brass and steel polishing, window cleaning, floor scrubbing, bedmaking, furniture polishing &c., &c. The Officers believe that this instruction, (in addition to cookery and laundry work taught in the Day Schools), will better equip the girls as domestic servants, and also render them more useful in their own homes.'

Much discussion in November 1899 was around the formation of an Amicable Society orphanage but it was realised that *'ample provision was already made for orphan children in the town'*. The matter was dropped in favour of increasing the number of scholarships and maintenance grants, providing classes in housework and supporting the pupils as they left school. They agreed that pupils could use their scholarships to attend the Higher Grade School that at the time was in the process of being built. Mr George Lord Beeforth was elected President in 1899 and 1900. Towards the end of 1900 a proposal was made to amalgamate the Society with the Scarborough United Scholarships Foundation. Mr Beeforth declared he was in favour of a total amalgamation when he was elected president for a fourth year.

On 4 December it was ultimately resolved:

'That the Officers of the Amicable Society approach the Governors of the SUSF with a view to amalgamation on condition that Higher Scholarships be established for the children of the deserving poor of the town.'

Mr Beeforth as President, Mr Raven, Mr Chapman and Mr Taylor were appointed to represent the Society when the charities met. They reported back to a meeting on 10 December saying that SUSF was willing to consult with the Amicable Society respecting the proposed amalgamation. Throughout the year adjournments and discussions on the matter appeared in the minutes. Clerk to the Magistrates, Mr H E Donner, of 38 Queen Street was the Secretary of the SUSF.

It would appear that a falling out between the President, George Lord Beeforth and William Ascough was narrowly averted. This was due to Mr Beeforth being unaware of a resolution to put off the Annual Meeting in June 1903 while they awaited the approval of the Charity Commissioners; he wrote a letter of apology to Mr Ascough, asking to withdraw his previous letter and saying:

'I should be most truly grieved if we should lose your most valued services... I earnestly hope you will remain with us until we join the Scarborough United Scholarships Foundation.'

Finally, as a result of the decision made at the Annual General Meeting of January 1901 where the officers:

'were empowered to consult with the Governors of the Scarborough United Scholarships Foundation, respecting proposed co-ordination or amalgamation for Educational Scholarships etc.'

and the meeting the following January when the officers:

'were authorised to approach the Charity Commissioners',

a meeting was held on 5 April 1904 to adopt the resolutions.

The Report was presented at a Special General Meeting in the Savings Bank in King Street on 21 October 1904 setting out the official resolutions:

1. 'That the Amicable Society be continued for the purpose of feeding and clothing the children of the poor of Scarborough.
2. That the cash in hand be retained for these purposes.
3. That this sum be invested in the names of the Officers, under Deed that the Interest only shall be used, and that in the event of the Amicable Society ceasing to exist, or the membership falling to less than 25, such principal sum revert to the United Scholarships Foundation
4. That it be referred to the Officers to submit new set of Rules applicable to the changed conditions of the Society
Completion of Scheme – The Scheme of amalgamation was sealed 20 June 1904, and after certain formalities was declared legal in September 1904.'

Under this scheme the Amicable Society was to appoint six representatives to the governing body of thirteen members, who would administer the funds for exhibitions from Elementary to Secondary or Technical Schools and for not less than two exhibitions tenable at any University, all these were to be applied for. The Amicable Society transferred to the Governors of the SUSF the school and houses and a capital sum of £7,105 10s 2d invested in Bank of England stock, all to be administered by the Charity Commissioners. It was estimated that the total income available would be about £425 each year. There was a sum of £800 in hand which had been invested in Scarborough Corporation Stock at 3.5% interest.

In the report, the Amicable Society Committee congratulated itself that now there was a ladder enabling even the poorest child in the town to climb to the highest educational position. They also acknowledged that 'to a starving child food is an even greater necessity than education.' During the previous two winters a system for free dinners had been set up by the Society, it had also been found that of the six thousand children on the school rolls, over two hundred were in need of food and clothing. Through the Amicable Society

'aided by willing hearts and ready hands, the poor and fatherless children may feel its benefit for many future years.'

Thanks were expressed to the President, Mr George Lord Beeforth for 'the most careful consideration' he had given to setting up the scheme with the Governors of the United Scholarships Foundation, the Charity Commission and the Board of Education. The printed document was presented on behalf of the Officers by the Honorary Secretaries, W Ascough and H Chapman.

The Scarborough Evening News of 22 October 1904 reported on this last Annual Meeting of the old regime held at the Savings Bank in King Street the previous day. Mr Beeforth had been unable to attend but he acknowledged the contributions of various bodies that had supplemented the Society's work, The Forty Club, the Mayoress who had started a fund and Messrs. Boyes who had done good work so that 200 of the town's 6,000 children had benefitted. The amalgamation with the Scarborough United Scholarships Foundation was now *'AU FAIT ACCOMPLI'* the paper announced.

Mr Ascough proposed the adoption of the new rules whereby the Amicable Society's work would be in clothing and feeding the poor children of the town. The Mayoress, Mrs Octavia Flora Morgan, had consented to become President, the first and only woman to be on the committee; William Ascough was appointed Vice President with Mr R Underwood and Mr H Vasey as honorary secretaries. The representatives to sit on the SUSF Committee for the ensuing three years were Mr G L Beeforth, who had been connected with the society for 57 years; Mr J Stephenson, 47 years; Mr R Smith, 34 years; Mr T F Taylor, 20 years; Mr H Chapman, 28 years and Mr Ascough, 20 years. So read the minutes of the short meeting following this Annual Meeting, the last one in William Ascough's distinctive handwriting that had filled two volumes of minute books and the last one to take place in the Saving Bank in King Street.

After the Amalgamation

How was the Amicable Society to fulfil its new role? The first meeting was in the newly opened Town Hall in St Nicholas Street on Friday 11 November 1904. Top of the agenda was the Provision of Free Meals. On the committee we find the Mayoress, Mrs Octavia Flora Morgan as President; William Ascough, Vice President; Wardens, Messrs T F Taylor, R Farrow, G W Boothby, W T Northorp, W Hutchinson, J Hind, J Geldorf and F G Pexton; Mr W Saynor, Treasurer; Mr

George Hankinson, Auditor and Secretaries Mr R Underwood, Mr H Vasey and Mr Henry Chapman.

In February 1902 the Society had given a grant of £5 towards the purchase of food tickets for distribution amongst the poorest children in attendance at the several Board and Voluntary Schools. Mrs Morgan, as President, reported that £26 12s 10d had been handed over to the Amicable Society from the Free Dinner Fund. At a meeting on 28 November they agreed to purchase Dinner Tickets on a weekly basis delegated to Mr W Hutchinson, a Warden, and Mr H Vasey, one of the Secretaries. It was also agreed to provide boots as *'many children are badly shod and during the winter weather boots are almost as necessary as food.'*

In December that year the Local Bandsmen paraded through the town collecting £17 for the Amicable Society, £7 of this was given to the Charity Organisation Society who were working alongside. The League of Social Service offered to investigate cases to guarantee that dinner tickets were given to the most deserving, there was even a suggestion of opening a 'Soup Kitchen'. The accounts list S Bailey and Albermarle Hotel and Cafe Co. as providers of meals in February and March.

According to the Report presented to the Annual General Meeting held in the Savings Bank on 30 October 1905, 13,788 dinners were supplied during the winter at a total cost of £114 18s 0d and some clothing had been distributed to cases in dire distress. Special thanks were given to the 'Forty Club' for raising £18 19s 3d at a Smoking Concert. One hundred listed subscribers gave a total of £42.18s. Miss Wood sent £3 2s from a collection held at Westlands School, they became regular contributors.

At their December meeting the committee decided to experiment with a Soup Kitchen at the St Thomas' School for the children in that school and the National School, other children would again be served by the Coffee Houses. Do we hear an echo of William's experience of hard times in Burnley? New methods of collecting money were tried.

Sunday 31 December 1905 saw a collection on the Marine Drive, supervised by Mr W Barham, the Chief Constable; it raised £5 9s 6d after 18s had been deducted for advertising. It is interesting to note that the Marine Drive was not officially opened until 1908, the first stone was laid in 1897 and the last one in 1904 but high tides and legalities caused delays. Prince Arthur, Duke of Connaught, performed the opening ceremony on 5 August accompanied by his wife and daughter, Princess Patricia.

Mr Taylor proposed a scheme to place collecting boxes in suitable shops; fifty boxes were ordered and in the first three months £5 12s 1d had been collected. As a result an order was made for another fifty boxes. Central Schools sent a donation of £10 from their concert. Further donations were received: £8. 8s came from the Scarborough Teachers' Association (NUT); £15 came from the Police Force Concert and £1. 15s Returned Income Tax from the Inland Revenue. The NUT was invited to send a representative to the Amicable Society Committee.

With renewed vigour the Committee set about raising money and support. In 1906 the Committee increased to include Mrs Brown and Miss Simpson from Central Schools, Miss C Cowling of the National Union of Teachers and three members of the Police Force, Detective Inspector George Nawton, Sergeant J Carter and P C Herbert Nalton. Mr J W Ness and Mr W Smith of Scarborough Forty Club and Mrs A S Tetley representing the Friends' Social Service Committee also came on board. The Municipal Secondary School raised £38 14s 6d at a Dramatic Performance and Concert. From H W Marsden's book we read that the scholars were going to donate their takings to their Sports Fund but Mr Tetley, the Headmaster, persuaded them to help these unfortunate children. The concert included Grecian Dances, an adaptation of 'Alice in Wonderland' and scenes from 'A Midsummer Night's Dream'.

The special subscriptions totalled £159 16s 3d in 1908 which included £20 from Lady Ida Sitwell's Special Distress Fund and £1 13 from Messrs W Rowntree's employees. £15

15s came from the Freemasons where William Ascough was a member. A guinea was raised at Central Boys' School from a lantern lecture, the forerunner of the slide show, £1 10s from Central Wednesday Football Club and the Reception Committee at the Journalists' Conference donated £13 15s 4d. In addition there were many contributions from various church collections. The lists appeared regularly in the Annual Reports, The Organization Committee held annual Whist Drives, in 1912 they raised the magnificent sum of £211 boosting that year's total to £279 2s 4d, the highest recorded.

1907 saw the effect of the Government's Education (Provision of Meals) Act 1906 when the Local Education Committee's desire to associate itself with the Amicable Society was agreed and the School Canteen Committee was formed. Members of this committee included the Officers of the Amicable Society, Councillor W Ascough and Councillor W Boyes from the Education Committee, Mr Daybell, an Officer of the NSPCC, and Mr Harrison of the COS.

The newspaper report on the Annual Meeting stated that the Committee felt the provision of free school meals was *'not a local matter but an Imperial matter'* and should not be paid for from the rates. The total number of meals provided was 13,238 at a cost of £94 9s 4d,

> *'this did not include an additional 1,000 dinners provided at the County Hotel by the Wanderers' Club and a number paid for at the Alexandra Restaurant by the President (Councillor Ascough)'.*

The Society had also spent £16 7s 9d on boots and clothing, twice as much as in the previous year.

William Ascough had retired from the Education Committee in 1905 and was elected to the Borough Council in the November representing the Central Ward. He was made Chairman of the Entertainments and Advertising Committee and worked with the Borough Engineer, Harry W Smith on the Alexandra Gardens and the Floral Hall project; the Gardens were opened on 27 June 1908. Was the President entertaining the children at this venue? William was elected Mayor of Scarborough in 1909 and in 1912 he became an Alderman. It was noted in the Annual Report of 1910 that when Mrs Ascough was Mayoress she had arranged for a weekly supply of milk for infants by placing about 100 tickets with the Society, Nurse Dunhill saw to their distribution.

William Ascough, during his time as Mayor of Scarborough

On 15 January 1908 the following were elected as representatives of the Scarborough Amicable Society on the Governing Body of the Scarborough United Scholarships Foundation: William Ascough, George L Beeforth Esq., Mr Richard Smith, Mr Thomas F Taylor and Mr R Underwood. Mr Beeforth was unable to attend so Mr Septimus Bland was elected in his place. We learn from the Annual Report that 34,812 meals were served during the 1907-8 Session at a total cost of £206 0s 2d.

> 'A sum of £15 14s 8d was paid by the Local Education Authority for services and provision of utensils &c.'

Meals were served until 31 March each year.

We are told that the providers of these meals were Bailey & Co., Wellburn's Cafe, Coffee House Co., St Thomas' Centre, Falsgrave Centre and Vollum's Cafe. The cost of each meal was no more than 1½d (a penny-ha'penny) Bailey's provided the most, over 15,000 and Vollums the fewest, only 240. New centres were added at Friarage and Claremont and in 1915 the Municipal School Centre was used which cost the Amicable Society £19 10s 0d. The winter of 1910/11 must have been particularly hard as the number of meals served reached 4,371, costing £245 12s 10d, the highest ever.

Strangely in 1914 – 15 only 6,308 meals were served and the School Canteens were not opened. It was suggested that

> 'with the liberal separation allowances granted by the War Office and the great number of fathers who joined the Army', families were better off.

The report for 1909 mentions:

> *If sufficient sums were available the work of the Society would be greatly extended as a Children's Care Society, providing in addition to meals, boots, clothing, and spectacles to poor scholars.*

Two years later we find:

> *Spectacles have also been supplied in very needy cases to children whose eyesight was defective.*

In 1911 the Annual Report is more specific under the title

'Other Care Work':
Aid was given in the purchase of spectacles where ordered by the School Medical Officer and the parents were too poor to provide. A sum of £2 7s 0d was spent in this work.

A sum of £46 6s 2d had been spent on Boots and Clothing, the boots were distributed in conjunction with the Local Police Force.

A letter entitled 'A Mother's Question' was printed in the Evening News on 20 January 1912. This mother's child had been refused a dinner ticket as he had not returned to school after having his dinner the previous day. He had gone home to wash his hands and face before returning to school but as his stockings were wet, through having bad boots, the mother had kept him at home thinking it wiser than letting him sit with wet feet all afternoon.

Hopefully the pupils liked peas when we read the sample menu given for School Canteen Centres, the nutritional value is debatable but the food would be filling:

'Monday - Meat and potato pie with peas or beans;
Tuesday - Potato and onion soup with dried green peas followed by rice pudding or wholemeal cake;
Wednesday - Stewed meat, suet puddings and dried green peas, bread;
Thursday - Minced meat with boiled rice followed by baked or boiled jam roll;
Friday - Pea soup and suet dumplings.'

Diversification

Over the years the Society diversified in the care it provided to the poor children of the town. Dr Knight, the Medical Officer of Health attended the Annual Dinner at the Balmoral Hotel on 13 December 1911. In proposing a toast he acknowledged the work the Society did and suggested that the ideals and conception of what education really implies had undergone a revolution; rather than as formerly cramming the memory with facts, it now meant drawing out and developing all the faculties of body and mind latent in the child.

The Society gave £20 for provision of an outfit for Hugh Lancelot Simpson who was emigrating to the Transvaal for health reasons in 1911, a year later they provided an invalid chair for Sidney Farrah who was to be admitted to a home in Croft near Darlington. Sadly the boy died there and the chair was returned. In 1913 a grant of 2s 6d per week was made towards the maintenance of Thomas Wilson, a 'cripple boy' aged 15, so he could be placed in *'some Institution where he could learn shoe making and become self-supporting'*. So many requests for boots and clothing had been made that in January 1913 a sub-committee was formed comprising the President, Mr Daniel, and Wardens, Mr J Jackson and Mr E H Matthews. Mr Matthews and Mr Underwood, the Secretary, were appointed representatives on the newly formed Scarborough Council of Social Welfare.

Somewhat poignantly given the date 31 July 1914, three requests were made for boys taking up careers at sea. James Appleby was granted £3 14s, being half the cost of an outfit as an apprentice in the Merchant Service; a sum 'not exceeding £7 10s' was awarded to Henry Owston who had secured a ship but his mother, Isabella, was unable to provide the requisite outfit and £20 was made available to Joseph Crathorne who was bound for the Training Ship 'Conway'. The Committee met on 16 November 1914, the day after the Bombardment of Scarborough, and considered an application from H Brown who was entering the Merchant Service and G Gospel who needed clothing to enter farm service.

The Society's Annual Dinners stopped in 1914 and the money from the Mayor's Banquet Fund, £16 16s was donated to the Amicable Society. In March 1915 the Mayor, C C Graham gave the Society £30 5s 1d that was left over from what was needed from the treats given at Christmas to the children of soldiers and sailors. In recognition Miss M B Graham, Mayoress, was made a Life Member of the Society as was Mrs P Cadman. Help was given to another recruit to the Merchant Service, Edgar Golder and to Jack Cattle, 'a deaf mute' who was seeking employment. He was successful in finding work in Hull with Mr D Hart and was granted 2s 6d per week to help support him, however, his master had been called up so Jack was put with Mr Coombes but he still needed help with his rent. At a later date Mr Jackson tried to find a position for him in Scarborough without success.

Mr G Colclough of the East Mount Sea Training School applied for assistance for four Sea Scouts who had gone to sea in 1917 and a further eight who left school in June 1918; each one was given £5 for their outfits. In this same year we find a young lady taking a new path, Margery Turner applied for help to attend Copley's Training School to learn Shorthand, Book-keeping and Typewriting, the Society agreed to pay £8 for the combined course.

We learn from the Annual Report of 1919 that the Society was working in close co-operation with the Medical Clinic, the Juvenile Employment Bureau, the Council of Social Welfare and the head teachers of the schools. The committee had considered helping the children who had lost fathers in the war and worked with Mr W M Stapley of the Local Pensions Committee. When they found these families were being supported from other quarters they realised that the mothers might benefit from their guidance when the children were 'ready to go out into the world.'

'Reversion to the Old Order of Things'

The Society continued in much in the same vein until 1925. The 'Provision of Meals Act' meant the Amicable Society's work had been taken over by the Education Committee and Councillor H Froggatt actually resigned as Vice-Chairman as that was what he was particularly interested in. With the Unemployment Insurance Act of 1920, many people could claim 'dole' thus cutting down dire poverty. The Annual Meeting on 24 February, Shrove Tuesday, saw the presentation of a framed photograph to Mr Josiah Wilson, the last head master of the Amicable School who was in post when William Ascough first came to the town. A reunion of old scholars had been held on 22 December and as a result Mr Wilson hoped many would become subscribers to the Society. He is quoted as saying *'it had been one of the pleasantest evenings he had spent.'* Alderman Matthews, the retiring President, hoped he would hang the photograph of the old scholars at the reunion in his room and live a long time thinking of them.

Alderman William Ascough, aged 76 and attending his 45th annual meeting of the Amicable Society, had accepted the invitation to become President because he had an important proposition to make. He felt that since the closure of the Amicable Schools, the Society

> *'had lost the personal touch with the children who should be the Amicable children of the town.'*

He recommended that the officers be empowered to appoint on the Foundation as Foundation children up to 12 boys and 12 girls who would be looked after in their homes and be in the personal care of the society. They would be entitled to be clothed and receive any required aid up to the school leaving age. The Scarborough Standard's headline on 26 February 1925 read: *'Ambitious Scheme Adopted. Reversion to Old Order of Things'*.

At the meeting on 26 June 1925 the first two scholars were elected, Arthur and Tom Appleby of 81 Hinderwell Road. There were also two daughters in the family, Sarah and Joan but the idea was that the money the family saved on the Foundationers could be spent on the other children. It was resolved:

> *(1) That Arthur Appleby (9) and Tom Appleby (8) be and are hereby placed on the Foundation of the Amicable Society.*
>
> *(2) For the first year a sum not exceeding £7 10s to be spent on each child and that in subsequent years a sum not exceeding five pounds per year be spent on each child. It was agreed that the first year's outfit should include two suits and an overcoat.'*

Mrs Appleby and her two sons were invited to attend the Society's meeting on 28 August 1925 when Alderman Ascough welcomed them to the Foundation. The Committee agreed to present each child with a Bible on entering the Foundation. Recorded in the minutes of the meeting on 30 October 1931 held in the Education Offices in Huntriss Row, a letter was read from Mr GKG Pindar, Tom's Warden, stating that:

> *'Tom Appleby of Field Side, Northstead, who attained the age of 14 years in January has now left school and is employed by Mr Little, a Dairy man in Beechville Avenue.'*

Although the committee wanted equal numbers of boys and girls, given the option, the mothers not unnaturally preferred the Society to clothe their boys, as girls could be dressed more cheaply. In 1926 eight more boys were added to the Foundation, they were: George Thompson aged 10, of William Street, the middle of nine children; Sidney Tyson aged 5, of Longwestgate, the middle of nine children ranging from 13 years to 3 days; John Place aged 13 of Lott's Yard, St Thomas Street, the fourth of ten children; Tom Haiking of Nelson Street, fifth of ten children; George Gibson aged 10 of Princess Lane, the second of seven children; Charles Moss aged 10, fourth of eight children; William Stockdale aged 11, second of seven children and Jack Kitchen aged 7, fourth of eight children living in Durham Street. The average weekly income for these families was around £2 10s, each with rent around 5 shillings. Ernest Agar was later added provisionally for a year but was kept on longer.

A ceremony was held in the Town Hall Council Chamber at the meeting of the Officers on 20 February 1926. Alderman Ascough referred to 'this beautiful room' in his speech to the boys and their mothers as he presented each child with a copy of the Bible. He encouraged the boys to read their Bibles, always to do their best and to be honest, upright and true. In keeping with earlier practices, he also suggested they may hold an outing in the summer time and a pleasant evening at Christmas. Sadly he was not able to organise either, as this was the last Amicable Society meeting he attended; he died on 12 July 1926.

The country was suffering the Great Depression when the Amicable Society celebrated its 200th year and although the Committee hoped to attract more subscribers, they were disappointed with the small increase. They decided to hold an Annual Dinner at the Pavilion Hotel at 7.30 on 26 March 1929; the cost was five shillings and six pence. At the Annual Meeting held in the Town Hall prior to the dinner, Mr Underwood took over as President from Mr F G Pexton, who became a Vice President together with Mr G W Boothby, Mr J Jackson and Mr W Saynor. The Wardens were Mr Sidney Fern, Mr G Mainsmith, Mr T Southwell and Mr J W Estill. Councillor Merryweather and Mr Lofthouse represented the Forty Club, the Secretaries were Mr R Underwood and Mr E I Baker while Mr W I Nelson was the Treasurer and Messrs Robinson, Coulson & Kirkby were the Auditors.

It is interesting to note that many of these gentlemen were longstanding members of the NUT. A book presented by the publishers Thomas Nelson 'A Guide and Souvenir' the first time the NUT Conference was held in Scarborough in 1906 has a chapter entitled 'Education in Scarborough', written by William Ascough, which includes information about the Amicable Society. Mr Estill, teacher at the

Municipal School, was Hon Secretary to the Conference Committee, Councillor Ascough was on the Benevolent Purposes Committee, Mr Pexton, Headmaster of St Mary's National School, Mr Fern who taught music at Central School and Mr Underwood, Secretary to Scarborough Education Committee, ran the Reception Committee. Mr Underwood had been the Headmaster of Gladstone Road Boys' School before becoming Assistant Secretary to William Ascough in September 1903.

Mrs Brown, Headmistress of Central Girls' School and Miss E H Cowling, Headmistress of Friarage Infants' School, were on the Ladies Committee and Mr A E Morley was Vice-Chairman to the Press Committee. It shows photographs of each committee member and Official, almost all the gentlemen sport moustaches and the ladies wear elegant high-necked dresses. The Scarborough Education Committee minutes of 6 March 1906 record Mr Estill asking permission to use some school premises as committee rooms for the NUT Conference. Perhaps we can assume that many of these people supported the Amicable Society over the years; the NUT still supports the Amicable Society.

Apparently out of the blue Mrs Reddin of Monmouth Lodge, Park Drive, Harrogate gave Mr J Jackson a cheque for £5 'to be devoted to some charitable purpose', reported in the minutes of 8 January 1932. Mr Jackson had suggested they provide an extra pair of boots as a present to each boy on the Amicable Society Foundation. Mrs Reddin was made a Life Member for her kindness which proved a good move as this kind lady offered to pay the cost of an outing for the boys in the summer months. The date chosen was 27 July and all the boys enjoyed a visit to Thornton-le-Dale, Kirkbymoorside and Helmsley. Mrs Reddin had also given money for book prizes for the three best essays about their visit. Captain Gibson, President, presented these books to Douglas Major, Joseph Hurd and John Watson. The same kindnesses were repeated in 1933 when the outing was to Whitby and Sleights on 31 July.

That summer three foundation boys left school, John Watson went to work in the Corporation Gardening Department, Douglas Major was employed by Mr Proctor, Plasterer and Builder, and Jack Kitchen had been offered a position as Page Boy at the Grand Hotel. William Ascough's wish for Summer Outings had been honoured.

The Christmas treat started up again in December 1942 when the Officers met up with the boys and girls on the Foundation and their parents at Grimstone's Cafe. This was less popular in 1946 so each of the four boys was given a book instead. Eight pupils attended a performance of 'Alice in Wonderland' at the Opera House in 1948, again in 1949, 1950 and 1951 the Opera House donated 12 tickets for the pantomime. Boots vouchers for 7s 6d were given by the Society to each child but in 1954 the Society decided to ask a local firm to supply the Christmas gift voucher; Messrs W Boyes & Co. obliged. Various firms have supplied these which are also given to any siblings in the family. Currently Boyes' Christmas vouchers at a discounted price are obtained annually from this same company. In 1962 the Ladies Auxiliary of the Licensed Victuallers Association treated the Foundationers to a trip to Billy Smart's Circus in Leeds.

The Amicable Society has adapted itself to the needs of pupils in Scarborough over the years when different Acts of Parliament have appeared. The 1944 education act was implemented in 1948 so the Amicable Society decided to cover children in Infant, Junior and Secondary Modern Schools while SUSF took on the Grammar and High Secondary Schools. More upheaval came with the arrival of Comprehensive Education in 1973 especially as the town lost its District Education Office and with it their secretarial services in March 1974. Traditionally the Education Office had provided all administration since William Ascough's time. Mr F Green agreed to be the Secretary and Mr Fred Robson, Headmaster of Braeburn Junior School offered to see the necessary typing and duplicating was carried out. From then on the Society has been run by volunteers.

After much discussion with the SUSF it was agreed in 1971 that the age demarcation line would be 11 years when the Foundationers would move from the Amicable Society's responsibility to that of SUSF but the Amicable Society Wardens would continue to see to their care. Currently the Amicable Society cares for all school children of families deemed to be in need, up to the age of sixteen. In addition to the twenty or so Foundationers who are taken on until they leave school or their circumstances improve; casual assistance can be given to any child who needs immediate help.

250 years on

The Old Butter Cross, Low Conduit Street

The Society celebrated its 250th Anniversary in 1979 with a dinner at the Royal Hotel on 30 March, a Service of Thanksgiving and Rededication in St Mary's Church on 1

April and an Art Competition sponsored by the directors of Scarborough and District Newspapers. It is interesting to note that at that time this group was owned by Sir Meredith Whittaker, grandson of Sir Meredith Whittaker, Chairman of the School Board and donor of the Whittaker Prize. The competition was on the theme of 'Children in Scarborough from 1729 to 1979' with classes for models, murals, drawings, paintings and a special section for the best examples of copper-plate handwriting. Lady Whittaker opened an exhibition of the winning entries at the Library on 31 March. Although no record was made of the winners, an interesting drawing of two ragged children waiting by the Butter Cross in Low Conduit Street for the Bellman to announce a vacancy at the Amicable School is reproduced on the Anniversary Dinner Menu; the artist was Catherine Sutcliffe of Graham Upper School.

The Royal Hotel served a dinner starting with Amicable Minestrone Soup followed by Yorkshire Pudding with Rich Onion Gravy, the Yorkshire way. The main course was Roast Sirloin of Beef with Horseradish Cream served with Buttered Brussels Sprouts, Roast and Creamed Potatoes. Next came Bronte Trifle, Wensleydale Cheese with Biscuits and Celery completed the meal. Mr Smith as President proposed the toast to 'The Queen', Councillor Harry Williamson responded to the Town Clerk, Mr Maurice Horspool's toast to 'The Mayor and Borough Council'. Mr Gilbert Gray Q C proposed the toast to 'The Scarborough Amicable Society'.

Gilbert Gray QC had been supported by the SUSF. His father was a butcher in the Bottom End and in 1946, after being accepted at Cambridge University, he applied for financial support. However Gilbert decided to do his Military Service first and took up his University Exhibition in October 1948 at Leeds University where he studied theology before switching to law. He was called to the bar in 1953 and became a Queen's Counsel in 1971. Over the years he developed an international reputation; cases he covered included the Selby Coalfield, the sinking of the 'Herald of Free Enterprise' in Zeebrugge, the Spycatcher case in Australia and hundreds of murder trials. He was probably one of the best examples of achievement by a beneficiary of the Scarborough Charities, a pupil who otherwise would not have been able to fulfil his potential.

The Service in St Mary's Church was conducted by Canon J Keys Fraser, Vicar of Scarborough, the Bishop of Hull, the Right Reverend Geoffrey Paul preached and twenty children from St Martin's C of E Primary School, dressed in the uniforms of 1729, paraded from Trinity House to the church. During the service they sang two hymns from the Amicable School Hymn Book, 'Jesu lover of my soul' and 'Praise the Lord ye heavens adore him'. The Mayor, Councillor H Williamson, read the lesson, Mark 10, 13 – 16 'Let children come to me...' The 'Litany of Thanksgiving' had been written by Maurice Horspool.

The Committee at this time comprised Mr Fred Smith, Headmaster of St Martin's School, President; Mr Frank Green, Secretary, he wrote a History of the Amicable Society in 1987, Mr R Fieldhouse had drafted an earlier text in 1963. Mr L Pickard, Treasurer, had recently taken over from Mr Maurice Horspool; Mr Fred Robson, Headmaster of Braeburn Junior School and Secretary of the SUSF following the death of Mr Clifford Morley; Miss Betty Foord, Headmistress of Burniston Village School, who later took on the role of Secretary; Miss Dena Hebditch, Headmistress of Braeburn Infants School; Mr JWF Wheeler, Headmaster of Newby Primary School. Mr Bob Bedford was Mayor the following year, he joined the Amicable Society Committee in May 1949 as the NUT representative when he taught at St Mary's National School, later he became Headmaster of Overdale Primary School before moving as Headmaster at Gladstone Road Junior School. In 1960 he took the place of Alderman GKG Pindar on the SUSF.

Another secretary-to-be, Mr John Morley, Deputy-Head at Gladstone Road Junior School, was on the committee. John's Father had died in March 1973 having served the Amicable Society since 1934. Mr Baker and Mr Halstead, the two Education Welfare Officers, were members of the committee and had a leading role in identifying possible children for consideration. Miss Sinclair, the retired Headmistress of Barrowcliff Infants and a past President, had recently died, Alderman Miles Bird, retired headmaster Northstead School had just resigned after 36 years' service to the Society. Dedication to the cause continues.

The Park Lodge Charity

Nestling in a folder labelled 'Constitution Documents Charity Commission' was a set of correspondence relating to the Park Lodge Charity. The letters had been sent to and from various solicitors and the Amicable Society and contained both the Draft and the sealed version of a Scheme dated 14 February 1974 concerning the Charity known as Park Lodge and the Charity of Dorothy Mary Chambers. The Trustees for the Park Lodge Charity were Ralph Kenway Rowntree JP of 245 Filey Road, Retired Company Director; Francis Leslie Tomlinson of 4 Cambridge Terrace, Dental Surgeon and Hannah Wallis JP of 5 South Avenue, Scalby, Married Woman.

Park Lodge began at 30 Gladstone Street in 1882 when a committee of ladies from the Female Mission decided to set up a home:

> *'founded for the training of little girls who were orphans or in circumstances of special need.'*

Perhaps this was one of the orphanages the Amicable Society had in mind when it decided not to set up on its own account. There were also in existence St Mary's Mission

House in Granby Place, St Martin's Rescue Home on Ramshill Road, Scarborough Refuge in Albermarle Crescent as well as Lady Sitwell's 'Home of Hope'.

The initial funds needed for furnishing and running this home were raised by four ladies who each promised £25. Their sub-committee set to work with the result that from its conception on 3 April it only took until 6 July to find and rent the house, at a cost of £20 a year plus £2 for the garden. They engaged a matron, Miss Hattersley, at a salary of £15. They also put an advertisement in the Scarborough Gazette appealing for subscriptions. The purpose of the home was to train the friendless little girls chiefly for domestic service.

More suitable premises for the home were purchased at 19 Park Street in 1899, for which they paid £400. It was reported:

'the close proximity to the Falsgrave Park and to the country lanes has been already a great advantage.'

From the details enclosed in the folder we read that during its 82 year history 178 children passed through the Home. It closed officially on 30 September 1964 when there were only three girls in residence, one left aged 18, another went to a foster home and the matron, Rena Champion continued to care for the remaining 14 year old.

Although not a Quaker foundation, throughout its history many of the Park Lodge Trustees were Quakers, including at one time Dena Hebditch. Dena recalls that the children attended Braeburn Infants School while she was headmistress from 1953 to 1963. Rena Champion was a most caring person and never missed a school event.

Miss Dorothy Mary Chambers was one of their first secretaries in 1882, she became President four years later and when she died in 1897, aged 92, she left 'a handsome legacy' to the home. It is possible this lady was born in Newcastle 1805, had been a governess to a family in York then had come to Scarborough to lodge with the Hawdon family in Alma Square. This family came from Blaydon and their daughter, Mary, was a Teacher Assistant in Scarborough. According to the Census of 1911, she became the Principal of a boarding school, 'Ravensworth Lodge' in Whitley Bay.

The first letter in the folder was sent from Pearsons and Ward, Solicitors of 7 York place on 26 October 1973, to D Harrison Esq., Secretary to the Amicable Society. Don Harrison was also the Scarborough Divisional Education Officer. This letter, together with the draft scheme, explained that the income from the Park Lodge Charity was to be shared between the Amicable Society and the National Children's Home, after payment of a pension to the former matron. Following her death the capital would also be similarly divided.

Mr Harrison duly replied accepting the scheme in December and also consulted Mr Maurice Horspool for an indication as to the value of this bequest. Mr Horspool, after speaking to the solicitors and one of the trustees, replied from his home address 178 Scalby Road saying he thought the Society would:

> 'get something over £200 pa which will go up to something over £300 when Rena Champion dies, which I understand she is not likely to do for some time.'

Meanwhile Pearsons and Ward received a letter from the solicitors Medley and Drawbridge at 74 Newborough to the effect that the Park Lodge Children's Home was to benefit from a sixth part in the will of HH Withnell Deceased. A list of 22 stocks and shares accompanied the letter. As the other beneficiaries had suggested the solicitors should sell these and share the money instead, the minutes of the meeting on 21 March 1974 noted that the committee agreed to fall in with them. Another letter from Mr Horspool calculates the valuation of this bequest *'something in the region of £8,000'* which is to be shared amongst the six recipients. He adds,

> *'Although it is of course a bad time to sell, it is a good time to reinvest.'*

Harry Withnell's father Charles had been a Bookseller, Stationer and Fancy Leather Goods Dealer at 4 Newborough since 1859. The name C J Withnell and Sons is listed as subscribing 5s to the Amicable Society in 1929. They had moved to Huntriss Row and sold out in 1945 so the Amicable Society continued to benefit from local businesses albeit in a round-about way.

In the next part we will take a closer look at some of the people who have worked for the Amicable Society and some of the children the Society has helped. They give us glimpses of what life was like in Scarborough over the last three centuries.

*

PART SIX
People connected with the Amicable Society

Henrietta Griffiths

Picture if you will a coach drawn by four long-tailed black horses, the coachmen proudly wear worsted lace livery while inside sit three well-to-do maiden ladies. Cutting a dash were sisters, Elizabeth Sidney Griffiths, Henrietta Griffiths and Anna Maria Griffiths of Barnborough Hall near Doncaster. They were regular visitors to Scarborough towards the end of the eighteenth century, staying at their lodgings 'Bell's Great House' in Longroom Street. Perhaps they met Mr Bell's daughter in her pink crinoline? One year, to pass the time possibly, they called in at the Amicable School and saw the pupils being taught Navigation.

They must have been very impressed as in 1840 their Solicitor, John Charge of Chesterfield, wrote to Dr Travis, of the Amicable Society, to ascertain that there were no other Charity Schools in the town where navigation was taught, before sending a legacy of £400. The youngest sister, Anna Maria, who had specially requested this money be given to the school, had died without a will in 1805. Mr Charge thought Anna Maria might have consulted Dr Travis while in Scarborough as she was 'out of health'. Miss Henrietta Griffiths had died in 1815 and had bequeathed 4/15 parts of £1,500 'at the decease of Harriet Barker'.

Dr Travis did his homework and was able to assure Mr Charge that *'"the long-tailed horses" are perfectly recollected'*. He consulted the schoolmaster who had taught at the school from 1798 to 1833 and was *'now aged about 75 and pensioned off'* who distinctly remembered the ladies visiting the school. He reiterates:

> 'at the date you quote, <u>at no other Charity School at Scarborough was Navigation taught</u>; With regard to the policy of educating Boys of that description for the Sea, it is gratifying to observe that very many have got forward so well, as afterwards to become Members of the Society to which they owed their advancement in life; - and some have risen to great opulence..

Dr William Travis painstakingly copied the whole correspondence between himself and Mr John Charge, some seven letters dated between 13 November and 28 November 1840, in the back of the Minute Book. The actual amount received by cheque on the Chesterfield Bank after the duty had been deducted was £360. The Special General Meeting held at the house of Mr Chapman, Old Globe Inn on Monday January 4th 1841 records:

> 'in order to determine upon the best mode of investing the legacy of the late Mrs Griffiths (a courtesy title) of Barnborough Hall, and that of the late Mrs Bowler of Scarboro' amounting together of upwards of £400 – also to consider the propriety of increasing the Number of Scholars.'

The decision was made that this amount together with monies invested in Dutch Bonds be transferred to real or Government securities and that future investments would not be put into foreign Securities. Three additional boys and one additional girl were to be admitted to the schools. A further legacy of *'Three Hundred and Thirty-eight Pounds, Thirteen Shillings and Twopence'* arrived in 1863 following the demise the other beneficiary from the will, Harriet Barker, who died without any children surviving.

Barnborough Hall was sold in 1859, at the Angel Inn, Doncaster on the death of the owner, Thomas Peter More. It was an Elizabethan mansion with an estate consisting of *'589 acres, 1 rood and 29 perches'* of farmland, several farmhouses and a water mill. Sadly after it had been taken over by the Coal Board it suffered subsidence and was demolished in 1969, all that remains is the dovecote, stable block and gardener's cottage.

The Mosey Family

William Mosey first enters the minute books as a Trustee of the Amicable Society in 1856 when Mr John Tissiman was the Chairman. The minutes of a meeting held at Mr Thirkell's Fleece Inn in January 1857 tell us that William Newham was elected as President, William Mosey, Samuel Bailey, Ingram Cockerill and Frank Ness became Wardens and the Trustees were Paul Lord, John Middleton, John Tissiman and Gilbert Wright. In 1858 Mr Richard Mosey appears as a Warden, he was a Trustee in 1859 and was elected President in 1860 during which time we met him at the Celebration Day. According to the Register of Members, Mrs Richard Mosey of 11 Falsgrave Road had become a subscriber in 1842. Other family members who already supported the Society include Thomas Mosey, 15 June 1835; Captain Mosey, 2 January 1837; Mr James Mosey, August 1837 and Mr Thomas Mosey, 4 April 1837. William Mosey had subscribed in July 1846.

Richard Mosey had presided over the appointment of a successor to Septimus Schollick at the special general meeting on 14 May 1860 at the Castle Hotel in Queen Street. Mr Thomas Archer was duly elected as schoolmaster with 143 votes, Mr James Gallie had 53 votes, Mr George Hunter 15 and Mr J J Dutton only 1. It had also been his duty to arrange the collection of donations, *'towards procuring a suitable testimonial for Mr Schollick'*.

In 1861 Richard was still a trustee and the following year he was on the Examination Committee list together with John Hebden (Treasurer), Dr W F Rooke, John Beckett, S Bailey and George Porrett. Richard Mosey appears on the list of those appointed to the Special Building Committee on

4 September 1862 with J Woodall as Chairman when arrangements were made to rebuild the Amicable Schools on the same site.

Each member was given an area of the town to collect subscriptions for the School Building Fund, Richard Mosey and Charles Hill were given Falsgrave. The Ladies connected with the Amicable School were allotted the task of holding a Bazaar as their contribution. That is the last minute in the book and sadly the next minute book in the archives starts in February 1889 so we have no further record of the Mosey family's connection with the Amicable Society apart from the name Captain Mosey in the subscribers' lists in the Annual Reports of 1900.

Why did this family sit along with the great and the good of Scarborough who served the Amicable Society? They were ship owners and master mariners living on Longwestgate. In the 1851 census William Mosey and his wife Helen, née Auld, born in Chesterfield, were at number 76 with their children Emma, born at sea in 1846, and William born two years later. At the same address we find Master Mariner George Batty (born in 1784) and his wife Elizabeth with their daughter, Ann Mosey and grandson Richard, born in 1844, although her address had been given as Falsgrave in 1842. Richard and his wife had moved to 8 Hinderwell Place their address in both 1861 and 1871 censuses.

By 1861, William, now a ship owner, and his wife Ellen had moved across the road to Number 71 Longwestgate, next door to Robert Tindall, ship builder and owner. William's family included Helen aged 9, John, 5, Frederick, 3, Arthur, 1 and Hessey, later called Henry, 1 month old. In the 1891 census, William Mosey, Master Mariner aged 49, was living with his wife Mary and their family at 28 Falsgrave, next door to William Ascough.

From an article about Frederick Mosey, written by Warren Bert Kimberley on the History of West Australia we discover something of their illustrious past:

> 'For generations the progenitors of Mr. Mosey fostered and stimulated marine mercantile expansion. Their fleets of merchantmen brought spices and rich balms of the East to England's shores, or laden with costly merchandise, traded to distant foreign lands. No less than five Captain Moseys, in command of their ships, met in one foreign port at the same time.
> Mr. Mosey's father, Captain William Mosey, shipowner, Scarborough, was widely known and highly esteemed among shipping circles. He conveyed the first church organ to Sydney, Australia. He also took the first railway material to the West Indies.'

Mr Kimberley mentions that Frederick's mother came from a Scottish family by the name of Auld and her father was known to Robbie Burns. Frederick spent some time at sea before turning his hand very successfully to commerce in Hull, York and London.

> 'Then he saw in the colonies a more elastic opening for his enterprising energies, and he sailed for Western Australia, arriving here on 5th April, 1887.'

He set up a land agency business in Perth and was instrumental in its early development.

In view of William Mosey's undoubted seafaring activities in the antipodes and William and Ellen Ascough's family connection with the Moseys, the present family still have some treasures William brought back from foreign parts, it may be a possibility that Ellen Ascough and her mother met Captain William Mosey when they sailed on their Tasmanian trip. They travelled out on the barque 'Dunorlan', a cargo boat, in 1863 under the command of Captain William Barwood, an English man who had settled in Launceston and married a Tasmanian. Then two years later Ellen and her mother returned to England on the

'Windward' with Captain Lulham. Both sailings are recorded in the Launceston Examiner of the time.

It is reported of Captain Barwood in his obituary in the Launceston Examiner of 31 May 1902:

> 'For a period of 33 years - from 1846 to 1878 - he made annual trips from London to Launceston, and vice versa, and during that period no more popular skipper visited the port. His commands included the barque Autannah, Dunorlan, Fugitive, and Lanoma, belonging to the firm of T. B. Walker, with whom he was connected all his sea-faring life.'

This makes the possibility of a connection even greater as Thomas Burlinson Walker was a Scarborough ship owner together with his son, a Master Mariner of the same name. In Pigot's Directory of 1834 they are living at 61 Longwestgate. They actually appear in the Amicable Society Minutes of 5th August 1860:

> 'Mark Almond had leave given to him to retire from the school, in order to be apprenticed to Mr T Walker, boat-builder.'

The Ascoughs had moved to Scarborough in 1879, the following year William Ascough became joint secretary of the Amicable Society. Could the Mosey connection have been an influence?

Charlotte Morley

In July 1855, S W Theakston, Bookseller of Scarborough sold for one shilling, a slender volume measuring four inches by six inches backed with a grey linen cover, to a young lady who wrote her name and address on the facing page, 'Charlotte Anne Morley, 12 York Place'. The title page tells us that it contains *'A collection of Psalms and Hymns for every Sunday throughout the year together with Hymns and Anthems for Special Occasions'* and was printed in Scarborough for the Amicable Society by J. Grice in 1850.

It begins at the First Sunday in Advent: for Christmas Day we find 'Hark the Herald Angels Sing' but on the first Sunday after Christmas, the children would be singing:

Short is the space to man allow'd
Before he must resign his breath
Exchange his beauty for a shroud
And sink beneath the hand of death.

Many of the hymns are still sung today but some might grate with today's political correctness. The hymn 'for the Anniversary Meeting of a Benefit Society' begins well enough with 'Our souls shall magnify the Lord' but reinforces the lot of the Amicable children and reflects the times they lived in:

Thou art our refuge in distress
The husband of the widow, Thou
The Father of the fatherless.

This book found its way into the archives so we need to ask who Charlotte was. Obviously not a pupil but she could have been on the Ladies Committee. Mr Geoffrey Knight was the President with Mr J W Woodall, Dr Cross, Mr J A Coulson and Revd J Oates as Trustees and Mr Thomas Allinson, Mr J S Thompson, Mr George Reynolds and Mr Septimus Andaer as Wardens. Miss E M Thirlwall had been appointed as mistress in March 1855 *'with the understanding her father Mr J S Thirlwall renders her his assistance in teaching writing and arithmetic'*; Revd Dr Whiteside had presided over the proceedings. At this time Charlotte would have been seventeen, two years younger than Elizabeth Thirlwell. Perhaps being an accomplished young lady she helped with teaching singing? Perhaps she was involved with the concert at the Spa on the Celebration Day in 1860?

There is no doubt Charlotte would have been well educated, she was the daughter of Francis Morley of Marrick Priory on the banks of the River Swale. Francis had succeeded his father Josiah in 1827 and married Charlotte Clervaux Chaytor of Spennithorne Hall near Croft in 1836. Their son, Francis, became Lord of the Manor on the death of his father in 1854 and sold the estate in 1895. Francis and his brother, Clervaux, both followed military careers: in 1881, Francis was in Dover with his Regiment as *'Lieutenant Colonel Commander 1/3 Foot the Buffs'* and in the 1891 census Clervaux, with the title Lieutenant Colonel R A, was living in a house in Woolwich.

Mother Charlotte moved to Scarborough with her daughters Anna and Alice, on the 1861 census they were lodging at Crescent Villa, opposite the Londesboroughs' summer residence and round the corner from Charlotte's address in the hymn book. Daughter Charlotte appears on this census as a visitor at Helmsley Lodge, home of Joshua Whitell and his family, three daughters and a son, Eugene, Lieutenant with the 2nd West Yorkshire Light Infantry.

If this had been an attempt at matchmaking nothing came of it, Charlotte settled in Scarborough with her mother and sisters. Their home in 1871 was 2 Gordon House on West Street, employing one domestic servant, but they had moved to 7 Grosvenor Crescent by the 1891 census, mother Charlotte was still with them, aged 80, and they had a cook as well as a housemaid. In 1901 we find only Charlotte and her sister Anna with their brother Clervaux, Colonel Royal Artillery (Retired), but ten years later Alice is with them and there is a cook and a housemaid in residence. Charlotte does not appear in any lists of subscribers or Ladies' Committees in the current archives of the Amicable Society so were it not for the hymn book we would never have met her.

Archdeacon Richard Frederick Lefevre Blunt

The connection between the Amicable Society and St Mary's Church was very strong under Revd R F L Blunt, later referred to as 'the Venerable Archdeacon'. He was appointed in 1864 and left in 1905 to take up the position of Bishop Suffragan of Hull. His first real contribution to the Amicable Society came when he was made head of the Committee of Revision. This committee had been set up at a Special General meeting on 2 April 1866 under Richard Cross, the President. He and the Wardens, John Woodall, Esq., A Gibson, Esq., the Mayor, W E Woodall, Esq., J P Moody, Esq., J Haigh, Esq. and S Bailey, Esq. assisted with the deliberations.

The first rule in this book which was published on 29 October 1866, concerns the Anniversary, *'to be held the first Wednesday after new year's day, at the school-room'*. The Members were to precede the children to and from St Mary's Church then, after the dinner *'at a house appointed,'* the Members were to elect four new Trustees *'by scratching on paper'*. The Ladies Committee was to be voted for in a similar manner, from the wives or daughters of subscribing members; their role was to superintend the Girls' School. The President was to be elected by the Trustees *'to preserve order'* and he was to have both the first and the casting vote. The Treasurer's job was to look after the monies and pay all dues under the written orders *'signed by the President and not less than two Wardens'*. He was also liable to pay any deficiency at the end of his tenure!

The Trustees for Cockhill Close were to receive the rents thereof and pay them over to the President, they also fixed the annual expenses of the processions. The trust deeds were to be kept in the iron safe at the School. The role of the Wardens was to see to contracts for clothing the children and to distribution of the funds *'on or before 28*

July' and to *'see each child be furnished with a bible and common prayer book'*.

Richard Blunt had been born in Chelsea in 1834; according to his interview in 'Some Scarborough Faces Past and Present' his father was one Samuel Jasper Blunt, a senior clerk in the Colonial Office. After being educated at Merchant Taylor's School, he studied law but decided to take up Theology at King's College, London. His first position was as a curate in Cheltenham then, following the death of Dr Whiteside, he was chosen as Vicar of Scarborough from four hundred applicants.

Richard Blunt and his wife, Emily, lived in the Vicarage, which was then at 7 Belvoir Terrace. Among the offices he held whilst in Scarborough were Archdeacon of the East Riding in 1873, Honorary Chaplain to the Queen in 1881 and Chaplain-in-Ordinary in 1885. He had been made a Canon of York in 1882 and five years later he was lecturing in Pastoral Theology at Cambridge University. From the evidence given in the interview, Dr Blunt was very busy: in addition to his work as Vicar, visiting the sick, opening three new churches, All Saints, St Paul's Mission Chapel and St John's Mission Church, he was also called upon by

> *'every institution in Scarborough which is doing useful and philanthropic work ... not because he was vicar, but because of his singularly good administrative parts.'*

This must have been true, from the list of organisations where he was chairman: the Society for the Prevention of Cruelty to Animals; the Society for the Prevention of Cruelty to Children; the Cambridge University Extension Society; the Literary Society; the Scarborough and Falsgrave Scholarship Trust Fund; the Teachers' Guild. He had a rapport with other denominations as he chaired the committee which presented a testimonial to Revd Balgarnie when he left the town to undertake mission work.

The 'Scarborough Faces' interview reveals the inevitable effect this had on him:

> 'The continuous and heavy work entailed by so large and important a parish, together with that belonging to his post of Archdeacon, made the Vicar feel the necessity of taking a rest.'

He took up the offer of the Chaplaincy of Christ Church, Cannes and spent the winter of 1881-2 in the South of France. Their family is listed in the 1891 census as: Edith, Hilda, Mabel, Arthur and Winifred. We do know that another son, Walter Brand Frederick Blunt was a curate of St Mary Abbots, Kensington; he died young as the Amicable Society members expressed their sympathy to Bishop Blunt at the Annual Dinner in 1898. Although Dr Blunt was appointed Suffragan Bishop of Hull in 1891, a newly created post, he continued as Vicar of Scarborough until 1905. The family moved to The Residency, Minster Yard in York where he died in 1910.

You may recognise the surname from a more recent news story. Their son, Arthur, also became a vicar, he eventually moved to Bournemouth where his son Anthony Frederick Blunt was born in 1907. This grandson became a leading art historian who, in 1964, confessed to having been a Soviet spy, one of the Cambridge Five with Kim Philby and Guy Burgess.

John Richard Halliday

This may not have been a gentleman of particular note but I find his story unusual. At their meeting in the Town Hall on 3 March 1905, Mr Underwood, the Secretary reported that he had received a cheque for £180 with instructions from the will of the late John Richard Halliday of Scarborough, a past President, who had died on 27 January 1879. Following the death of his wife, £200 (less £20 in legacy duty) was to be paid to the Trustees of the Scarborough Amicable Society's Schools for them to invest:

> 'as they may think fit, and the annual sum of ten shillings, part thereof to be paid by them to the Burial Board for the purpose of keeping in good order and condition the piece of ground in the Scarborough Cemetery purchased by me of the said Burial Board and my tombstone that may be placed thereon, and the residue of such interest shall be from time to time applied towards the maintenance or for the benefit of the said Schools.'

The Trustees gratefully accepted the legacy and paid £7 10s for proper maintenance of the grave in perpetuity. Mr Halliday had been an auctioneer and lived at 13 Granby Place in Queen Street, his property may even have backed on to the Amicable Schools. He had a wife and a daughter, both called Henrietta. He is described in the report of 1905 as 'a very old and loving friend of the Society'.

In November 1912 a request was made from the cemetery for repairs to be made to the monument and Mr Lomas' offer to do the job was accepted. Eight years later, the President, Mr J Jackson was requested to visit the memorial with the Secretary, Mr Booth. As a result, minuted on 17 June 1920, Mr Webster was asked to renovate it at the cost of £6. Mr Jackson was not satisfied with the work when he went to inspect it in the September and decided that the account would not be paid until he was satisfied. In April 1952 tenders for putting Mr Halliday's grave in order were obtained from three firms, that of F Dove and Son was accepted amounting to £21 12s.

Octavia Morgan

Octavia Flora Morgan's signature appears six times in the Amicable Society's Minute Book between 1905 and 1906 in the office of President. Why should this be considered noteworthy? She was the first woman ever to sit on the committee in the Society's 176 years history.

How she came to be a member of the committee let alone its president is something of a mystery. Her husband, Councillor William Morgan, was the Mayor of Scarborough three years running from 1902 to 1905 and he took the chair at the momentous Annual Meeting on 21 October 1904 when the Amicable Society amalgamated with the SUSF. The report on the meeting in the Scarborough Evening News tells us that, amid applause, the Mayoress had consented to become President. Her first signature sits under the pasted-in copy in the Minute book with William Ascough's handwritten comment *'taken as a correct Record of the Proceedings of the Annual Meeting held Oct 21 1904'*. She also appears on the list of subscribers as donating 5s in 1905 and £1 the following year.

William Morgan was a colourful gentleman described as *'portly, bespectacled and bewhiskered'*. He had come to Scarborough in 1886 to run the Aquarium, also known as Gala Land, whilst still managing the Winter Gardens in Blackpool. He was a widower when he married Octavia in 1885, she was 23 and he was 55, just three years younger than her father. They were married by Revd Charles Pakes in St John the Evangelist Church, a stone's throw from the Winter Gardens 'by licence'; he was not the regular Vicar.

Perhaps we can shine some light on Octavia's interest in education if we look at Revd Charles Pakes. He had been the Curate at Christ Church, Blackpool in 1871 and was a master in the Chalgrove Academy, later named the Collegiate School, next door to the Winter Gardens. He moved to Copp Church in Great Eccleston in 1880 which had a charity school so perhaps William and Octavia had connections with him through this work?

William Morgan was born in Staffordshire but his family moved to Bradford where they ran a large news agency. He became interested in bringing nationally acclaimed companies to theatres in Bradford, one such being the Carl Rosa Company. Eventually, together with three friends, he built his own Princess Theatre, where they combined theatre with music hall. Sadly this theatre burnt down and he eventually moved to Blackpool via Morcambe in 1880.

The Aquarium in Scarborough had been considered a white elephant as an exhibition of marine life; it was extremely lavish, built to look like an Indian temple, and had cost a total of £120,000. The underground site at the sea end of the Valley covered 2½ acres and was lit by 1,600 gas jets. William Morgan and two friends bought the building and its fittings for £5,150 in 1886, whereupon he and Octavia moved to Scarborough in the August. Mr Morgan was very enterprising and knew how to entertain people, he is quoted as saying, *'people would rather see a juggler than an uncooked lobster'.*

He brought variety to Scarborough. For a mere sixpence people could enjoy a ten hour programme of concerts, variety shows and swimming entertainments in the renamed 'People's Palace and Aquarium'. Among the attractions we find Captain Webb and 'an ornamental swimmer' called Ada Webb, not related to the Captain, who smoked cigarettes under-water. Carl Unthan, an armless concert violinist, entertained and there was an exhibition of lions, tigers, monkeys and exotic birds. It was not long before William Morgan was elected to the Borough Council. In 1902 his first mayoral year, he became President of the Scarborough Hospital in Friars Way and presented the Hospital Cup to the Bowling Club.

His wife's background was quite different. Octavia's father, James Firth, was in the family business of manufacturing woollen blankets in Liversedge, Heckmondwike, although he had retired at the age of 44. The family with at least six children lived at Spring House, they employed a governess, a cook, a waiting maid, a nurse and two housemaids, all resident. I wonder under what circumstances she came to meet William, did Octavia enjoy the delights of Blackpool's Winter Garden?

When they first moved to Scarborough the Morgans stayed in lodgings in St Nicholas Street according to the 1891 census. These were run by William King, a confectioner, and his wife Sarah, their four children were all confectioner's assistants. Could this have been the same popular establishment owned by Mr Bell, confectioner from York in 1804? By 1901 they were living at 9 Valley Road with a cook and a housemaid, they had no children.

From February 1905 to October 1906, the time when William Ascough was elected to the Council and Octavia was President of the Amicable Society, she also attended meetings of the Education Committee. The newspaper report for 17 December 1906 tells us, however, that Mrs Morgan was prevented from attending the Amicable Society's Annual Meeting *'owing to the indisposition of Mr Morgan.'* He died on 22 April 1907 and the census of 1911 reveals Octavia Flora Morgan was staying in a boarding house in Bath, a widow on Private Means.

George Lord Beeforth

Mr Beeforth appears in the Amicable Society list of *'Members' Names with Dates of Admission'* in 1847 when his address is given as Neasden House, Middlesex N.W.; later his address appears as Belvedere, Esplanade. His service as a Trustee was from 1881 to 1883 and he became President in 1899. At the time of the amalgamation with the SUSF, George Lord Beeforth was very involved in the negotiations, possibly because he had benefitted from an education which led to a lucrative career through someone else's kindness and he wanted to see others have the same opportunity. Perhaps his best known legacy to Scarborough is the beautiful landscaped garden on the South Cliff, particularly the Rose Garden, also known as the Rosary, with the cliff walks.

George Lord Beeforth was born on 31 March 1823 to Captain George Beeforth and his wife Susanna. He was baptised by Revd Samuel Bottomley who served the Independent Church in Eastborough from 1773 to 1830. George was the only boy in the family; his sisters were Hannah, Elizabeth and Jane all older than him then came Susan, three years later. After their father retired from the Merchant Navy, having fought in the Peninsular War, he opened a grocery business in Long Room Street but died in 1833. Susanna, a widow aged 52, had difficulty financially and ran a boarding house. A cousin, Revd Joseph Skelton, Vicar of Wold Newton, paid for George's education at the Grammar School, which at that time would have been run by William Merry in King Street.

On leaving school, George was apprenticed to a bookseller. In 1848 the Revd Skelton came to his aid, he provided the capital to enable him to set up his own business as a librarian and bookseller in St Nicholas Street, previously Long Room Street. By 1861 George was living in Belle Vue Terrace with his wife Helen, ten years his senior, and their son Henry aged four; his sisters Hannah and Elizabeth were also in residence.

He retired from his Scarborough business in 1866 and was elected to the Borough Council for two years before joining up with a friend, Mr Fairless, in Bond Street where they published line engravings. The family address in 1881 is 14 Buckland Crescent, Hampstead. The company employed the best engravers in France and England, one being Gustav Doré; a plate of the Holy City was probably their most famous engraving. They sold the business to the Doré Gallery Company in 1889, the building was later taken over by Sotheby's. When the family returned to

Scarborough, George took his place on the Borough Council and was made Mayor in 1893.

With the proceeds of his success in Bond Street, George spared no expense on their new home 'Belvedere' on the Esplanade. The South Cliff was a rapidly growing area for the well-to-do. George acquired a large stretch of land with an outlook over the sea and a private tunnel under the road to access the cliff. He laid out a large area as garden and woodland to further his hobby, collecting exotic trees. Proving the experts wrong, he grew many evergreen shrubs by the sea.

'Belvedere' was built in the Elizabethan style but with the most up-to-date accoutrements including electric light. In his library was an organ that was operated by piped water, the mechanism was hidden under the floor and behind the books. His bookshelves contained many first editions including Thomas Hinderwell's 'Histories of Scarborough'. As well as the library, there was a drawing room, a dining room and a billiard room, all beautifully furnished and decorated to the highest taste. He had commissioned James Ward Knowels of York Minster to install fifteen stained glass windows on the landing depicting Psalm 150 'Let everything that has breath praise the Lord'. At the time the editor of the Scarborough Magazine visited, around 1901, George Beeforth was busy compiling a volume of his own with portraits, old engravings and maps to do with people of note in the town.

In the census of 1911 he was a widower living at 66 Esplanade, his sister Elizabeth was still living with him and they had been joined by his granddaughters, Beatrice aged 29, born in Edinburgh and Gabrielle, 23, born in Remo, Italy. There was also a visitor, Ernestina Kloss of Arnsberg, Westphalia and four female servants.

Simpson Parkinson

'The London Illustrated News' was a publication started by the Ingram Family in 1842 and continued as a weekly paper until the 1970s, it came out on Saturdays and covered items of interest from all parts of the country. The edition of 2 June 1860 had an article entitled 'The Recent Storm' referring to the previous Sunday and Monday, 27 and 28 May which happened to be Whitsuntide. In addition to the ships that had been damaged in Shoeburyness, Yarmouth and on the river in London, some hundred vessels lost and their crews perished, fourteen fine elms were blown down along the Ouse at York. We also read:

> 'At Scarborough, a hairdresser, named Parkinson, while at breakfast felt the house rocking, and rushed up to get his children, who were still in bed. A stack of chimneys fell as he was going and killed him on the spot. His wife and children were extricated unhurt.'

David Parkinson had been a publican when he and his wife Ann set up home on East Sandgate, their family included Stella, who had baby Margaret in 1861 and was living at home, Alan, Isabella, Charles, Edward, Simpson born in 1854 and Robert born two years later. David became a hairdresser and they moved to 7 Globe Street, named after the Old Globe Inn. Their neighbours included a jet cutter at number 8, a jeweller at number 3 with a skin merchant next door while a baker and a greengrocer lived at numbers 11 and 12.

Fortunately for Simpson Parkinson, we learn from the minutes of a Special Meeting held at the Globe Hotel on 15 December 1862, the Amicable Society decided to award him a place at their school. The Old Globe Inn was one of the oldest inns in the town, it had been used by farmers coming to market, later it was popular with the nobility visiting the Spaw. There is a record of its fare in 1733, fish, rabbits, mutton and poultry were among the ten to twelve dishes served at 2 o'clock, Spaw waters were supplied with wine to wash it all down.

In line with the custom of the Amicable Society, Simpson was given a trade; he became a plumber and glazier. He married Mary Hannah Birley on 28 October 1882 and in the 1911 census Simpson was still a plumber, living at 26 North Street with his wife and family plus his niece Barbra. The Bible that was presented to Simpson is in the archives, it is inscribed in beautiful Copperplate writing,

'To Simpson Parkinson on his leaving the school of the Amicable Society November 2nd. 1868. Hodgson Smith Esq., President.'

The family has kept a note of births and deaths in the front cover so we know their first child Gertrude Ann born in 1883 only lived for two years, Alan was born in 1885, Charles in 1887, another Gertrude in 1889, Nellie in 1891, Simpson in 1894, Lillian (who may have written the information) in 1896 and Edith the youngest in 1898. On 1 September 1928 Lillian married Thomas Steel who died on 26 August 1956; she later married Herbert Mallinson who died on 1 December 1965. In different handwriting we find Grandson William Parkinson, son of Alan, married Charlotte Hardy on 18 August 1933.

William Tindall

In Scarborough the name Tindall is synonymous with shipbuilding. Tindalls had taken their place among the Burgesses and Bailiffs in the Common Hall for hundreds of years. In 1834 William, James and Robert Tindall are listed as Shipbuilders on Sandside, James and Robert lived next door to each other at 68 and 69 Longwestgate while Joseph Tindall lived at number 23. Robert was the last of the shipbuilders in Scarborough. John Tindall lived at Cliff, as

St Nicholas Cliff was then called, and was a banker. His son William, born in 1826, was lost in another storm tragedy that occurred in November 1861 and is well documented by writers and artists alike.

Around mid-day on 2 November a hurricane hit the town causing mountainous seas. The previous night, Pilot William Leadley had escorted the Scarborough boat 'The Wave' back to harbour and set out again but that was the last that was seen of him. Another boat, 'The Harbinger' was wallowing some four miles away while a schooner 'The Coupland' from North Shields, trying to make the treacherous entry to the harbour, got into difficulties off the Spa. Although Scarborough had run its own lifeboat since 1801, one of the earliest in the country, the Royal National Lifeboat Institution did not take it over until 1861 when the first lifeboat 'Amelia' was put in service.

With the regular lifeboat men already at sea, a scratch crew set out in this new boat. It was buffeted against the Spa Wall and two of the lifeboat men, John Burton and James Brewster, were thrown into the sea and drowned. 'The Coupland' was totally wrecked but all her crew were rescued by rocket lines that were fired successfully from the Spa building. Many people rushed to witness the scene and some spectators tried to rescue the lifeboat men but lost their own lives in the attempt. Lord Charles Beauclerc, soldier, artist and brother to the Duke of St Albans, was one such as were John Isles, a shoemaker, and William Tindall, shipbuilder and father of five sons.

Mr Oliver Sarony, a renowned photographer in the town, also joined in the rescue. He was more fortunate and survived the ordeal although it took three hours to resuscitate him. The RNLI awarded a Memorial Silver Medal to Sir Charles Beauclerc and William Tindall and a Silver Medal to Oliver Sarony among others. Mr Sarony commissioned his friend, Paul Marny to paint a picture of the shipwreck based on this tragedy.

However, the William Tindall who attended the Amicable School and received the two books, 'Old Transome' and 'The Admonitions' already mentioned, cannot have been part of the wealthy family with whom he shared a name. It would appear that he was the son of another John Tindall, a carrier from Yedingham, his mother was called Tamar. In 1871 they were living at 15 King Street where John was a milk dealer. William, born in 1865, had an older sister, Ann, three younger brothers, George, John and Frank, and two younger sisters Eliza and Tamar. By 1871 William's mother, now a widow, had taken a job as a charwoman and they were living in Providence Place.

Like Simpson before him, William was given a trade on leaving the school, he became a plumber. He married Louisa Priestly in 1890 and had a son, William, and two daughters, Louie and Ella who were all living at 66 Raleigh Street in 1911.

John Jackson

As a baby, Johnny Jackson arrived in Scarborough by boat in a basket carried by Mary, his mother, so it is said. He was born in Middlesbrough in 1874 and entered the Amicable School in 1881. On the census of that year he was living with his mother at 1 Friars Gardens. Mary was a dressmaker who originally came from Sherburn. The family included his sister Mary, aged 9, and brothers James, aged 4 and Tom just 2 but there is no mention of their father, James. It is possible his brother James also attended the Amicable School as *'a boy James Jackson was presented with a Bible on leaving school'* in 1890.

At the age of 12, Johnny was apprenticed to a tailor and was paid 2 shillings a week. He must have learnt well as he opened a shop at 9 -10 Queen Street as 'Tailor, Clothier and Boot Factor'. He married Zillah Stephens, whose family was living at 58 Franklin Street, having moved from Worcester. By 1911 they had four sons, Ernest born in

1895, Percy in 1898, Clifford in 1901 and the youngest Bernard born in 1904. Johnny sold ready-made suits for 30 shillings and a pair of boots cost 10/6: all the family lived in the flat above the shop. His mother, Mary Jackson, died in 1912

The Maritime Heritage Museum has an account of their eldest son Ernest who had gone to St Martin's School after leaving Friarage and in 1911 was working as a tailor and outfitter in his Father's shop. He enlisted in the army at the beginning of World War 1 in 5th Yorks at their headquarters in North Street. He wrote home on 25th May describing the bullets flying through the trees. He was killed the following day at Zoovre Wood near the Flanders village of Hooge, a shell had burst in their trench. 'D' Company Commander, Major Cyril Harvey Pearce, wrote to inform Mr Jackson of the death of Lance Corporal Jackson saying how sorry he was to lose such a capable young soldier. Ernest's name is inscribed on the Menin Gate as one of those missing at Ypres and on the family gravestone in Manor Road Cemetery.

Mr J Jackson is described as 'larger than life' even though he was small, he was dapper and sported a waxed moustache. He was elected as a Warden to the Amicable Society at the Annual Meeting held in the Town Hall, St Nicholas Street on the afternoon of Thursday 26 November 1908. He became the President in 1918 thereafter alternating between President and Vice-president, continuing as a Warden and in 1924 he was appointed Secretary on the resignation of Mr Dobson. He served on the 'Boots Committee' and regularly supplied outfits for the children even during the war. In the minutes of 17 December 1942, the amount in payment for Clothing and Boots was £61. 3s.5d. We read in the Minute Book:

'that the best thanks of the Officers of the Society be extended to Mr J Jackson for the excellent supply of

boots and clothing he has been able to obtain during the past year in the face of very great difficulties.'

John Jackson had been elected to the Town Council as a Liberal in 1924 and became Mayor in 1945. The Amicable Society presented an illuminated scroll to him at a Special Meeting of Officers at the Education Offices on 6 November:

'to place on record the sense of satisfaction with which the Society regarded the election of Councillor J Jackson as Mayor of the Borough.'
They were all aware that Councillor Jackson never ceased to glory in the fact that he was an Amicable Schoolboy... he had by his loyal and devoted service repaid that debt a thousand-fold,'

This was the comment made by the President, Mr S V Fern who signed it together with the Secretary, Mr H V Willings and his assistant Mr Alfred Quick; Mr W Curtis, Treasurer; Wardens: Mr S D Brown, Mr J S Rawlings, Miss Adelaide Trail, Mr J W Estill, Mrs Lily Harland, Mr John Jowsey, Mr L H Thompson, Jenkinson Riby, Mr E I Baker (an Amicable scholar with John Jackson), Mr T E Thornton, Mr A Clifford Morley and Mr Miles E Bird. Three of the current Foundationers were also present, 'to preserve the link between the old and the new', two signed the scroll, Robert Sweeting and A Casper. The signatures are difficult to decipher as the ink is now very faded. Robert lived at 9 Longwestgate and Mr Morley was his warden. Mrs Harland JP presented Mrs Jackson, the Mayoress Elect, with a bouquet of chrysanthemums.

In the Minutes of 24 Jan 1952, Mr J Jackson proposed to entertain the Foundationers to tea during the current year, being the Jubilee year of his being in business on his own account. The celebration, enjoyed by Officers and Foundationers, was held on 1 April. Mr Jackson later became an Alderman but kept his contacts with the

Amicable Society. John Jackson died in 1953, Zillah had died in 1950. He was a member of St John Ambulance and John remembers parading with him as a Cadet. Their son John was well known as a sea-angler.

Ernest Trott

Scarborough has naturally had strong connections with the sea so it is no surprise that the Amicable Society helped many boys to become seafarers. One such was Ernest Trott who had been attending Falsgrave Board School. At a meeting held in August 1900 Mr W Ombler, who joined the committee in 1896, proposed:

> *'That a grant of £10 be made to Mr Trott, in aid of outfit necessary for the boy to avail himself of the Scholarship won; with a further promise of a similar grant should the report respecting his behaviour and success at the end of the ensuing year be satisfactory.'*

Ernest Trott, born in 1886, had been awarded a County Council Scholarship value £42 per annum for 3 years, this was a Nautical Scholarship on the Training Ship 'Conway'. The family lived at 74 Highfield, off Seamer Road, father Thomas was a journeyman joiner, Ernest was the eldest child then came Florence, Ethel, John, Edith and Thomas. On his earnings of 30 shillings a week Thomas could not afford the £20 needed for the uniform as well as travelling and other expenses. A further grant of £5 was given in January 1902 then on 15 July 1902, we read in the minutes that Ernest:

> *'had completed his training with great credit; having obtained the Gold Medal for greatest efficiency and also obtained six other prizes in the final examination. He had been appointed as fourth officer in one of the great steamship companies and also been appointed by*

the Lords Commissioners of the Admiralty as Midshipman in the R.N.R.'

The committee made another grant of £26 to Mr Thomas Trott to enable him to purchase the outfit his son needed to enter his profession. Mr Trott's gratitude was expressed in a letter addressed to Mr Ascough, dated 15 August 1902:

'Dear Sir,
Will you kindly convey to the President and Wardens of the Amicable Society my sincere thanks for the gift of £26 which they have so generously voted my son Ernest for his outfit.

I am pleased to hear that his progress on board the Conway is considered satisfactory, as without the help so kindly given by the Society he would not have been able to take up the Scholarship, so that whatever position he may eventually rise to he will owe it largely to the Amicable Society.

I hope he will ever gratefully remember the obligation he is under to this Society and trust that he will someday be able to refund the money so generously advanced.

I beg to thank you personally for the interest you have taken in my boy and the help and advice so freely given whenever I have had occasion to ask for it, also for the kindly expression of good wishes.
I am,
Yours very respectfully
Thos. M. Trott'

We move on thirteen years to 14 July 1915, with the country at war. The Amicable Society held its meeting with Mr A M Daniel JP, the President; Alderman Ascough JP and Mr H Vasey, Vice-Presidents; Wardens Mr G Boothby and Mr J Jackson and Mr R Underwood, the Secretary. An *'interesting letter'* was read from Ernest Trott, Marine Superintendent of the Steam Navigation Company, Calcutta with a cheque for £20 enclosed

> *'which covered the amount (£16) which he had received, the balance being considered as interest.'*

The Officers were *'very gratified ... as he was under no obligation to return anything'* and promptly elected Ernest Trott a Life Member of the Amicable Society.

At that time the Steam Navigation Company in Calcutta was transporting the British Expeditionary Forces from India to fight in the war in Europe. They were also sending hospital ships, the 'Rohilla' that was wrecked off Whitby Harbour in December 1914 being one such. Ernest Trott had done well and duly showed his gratitude to the Amicable Society.

The Forty Club

In 1899 the Forty Club met in the Balmoral Hotel 'for the intellectual advancement and entertainment' of its forty members and with the intention of doing 'good works' for the Amicable Society and other worthy causes. Their first Annual Smoking Concert was held on 12 March 1900 when around 100 guests enjoyed an excellent musical programme. In 1903 their proceeds were devoted to providing free dinners for necessitous children. The following year Mr W Ascough spoke to the members calling attention to the Education Committee's free dinner scheme for poor children with the result that another 'Smoker' was held for which a piano was hired for 4 shillings.

In 1905 the Society received receipts of a Smoking Concert, given by the "Forty Club", £18.19s.6d. Two years later Mr T W Ness and Mr W Smith were appointed as representatives of the 'Forty Club' on the Amicable Society Committee. The club maintained its connection with the Amicable Society. Mr Estill, who was also a member of the

NUT, was a long-serving member on the committee as were Mr Lofthouse and Mr Mainsmith. From April 1930 a Mr S Boyes was one of their representatives; he was elected President in 1936.

*

PART SEVEN
The John Kendall Trust

The Charity in 1941

The John Kendall Trust is a comparative newcomer on the list of our Scarborough Children's Charities, it was sealed by the Charity Commission on 11 November 1941. The application had been made by the Reverend Canon Charles Patteson, Vicar of St Mary's Church from 1937 to 1944. Two other Trustees, the Mayor of Scarborough, John Cecil Ireland of 4 The Crescent, and Sydney David McCloy, Solicitor, of 38 Queen Street had been present when the resolution was passed and the other three trustees had been informed by post. They included the Reverend John Wynyard Capron who was living in Oxted, Surrey, he had been the Vicar of Scarborough from 1923 to 1930, and the Venerable Anthony Basil Carter, Vicar of Scarborough from 1930 to 1937, who had moved to Stokesley as Archdeacon of Cleveland.

The third was the Reverend Charles Edmund Swinnerton of Sessay who may have had an interesting connection with the Kendall family. He was born in 1882 in Streatham, the son of George Isaac Swinnerton, Curate of Immanuel Church, and his wife Bessie Kate. He had two brothers, George and Herbert and a sister Kathleen. According to Crockford's Clerical Dictionary he gained his MA at St John's College, Oxford in 1907 and became a curate at St Matthew's in Bethnal Green.

After the First World War he took the post as Vicar in Muston for a year before moving to St Thomas with St John in Scarborough. The St John the Evangelist mission church, one of three commissioned by Revd Blunt, had been built in 1883 on the corner of St Sepulchre Street and Globe Street. Perhaps Simpson Parkinson's house was one that was knocked down to make room for it; it closed in 1939. In 1924 Revd Swinnerton went to Nottingham to the church of St John and St James; he was Rector of Sessay near Thirsk from 1928 and died in Agbrigg, Wakefield in 1940.

The Swinnerton family has compiled a record of their history which, in Volume 11 produced on 12 April 2002, relates the story of Revd Charles Swinnerton. Apparently he decided to be a missionary in North Borneo during the First World War but unfortunately could not afford the return fare to England for himself, his wife Grace and their son Charles Guy Dover. With great ingenuity, he borrowed the sum of £38 from the government of Hong Kong in 1918, having obtained the permission of Major-General Ridout, General Officer Commanding South East Asia, with a view to answering the call to serve his country in the Guards. When the Army realised that Borneo was not attached to the continent of Asia, they found they were not authorised to pay the money. It took until April 1920 to sort it all out. There is a record of Mrs Swinnerton's experiences in Borneo in Owen Rutter's 1922 book 'British North Borneo'. In a particularly beautiful area of the country there is a high and almost inaccessible mountain, Kinabalu. In 1916 the intrepid Mrs Swinnerton climbed it to have a picnic. Their son, Charles Guy, was the last in this line of the family to become a Vicar.

Back to the John Kendall Trust. The charity was

'founded by 2nd Codicil to Will proved in the Principal Registry on 10th May 1923.'

The Trustees were to be *'seven competent persons'*. The Mayor of Scarborough for the time being was the ex-officio Trustee, representative trustees were to be appointed

'one by the Scarborough Local Education Authority; and one by the Vicars for the time being of the Ecclesiastical

Parishes of St Mary, St Thomas and All Saints, Scarborough'

each to serve for four years. In addition there were four Coöptative Trustees, each to serve a term of five years. The first named Trustees were the Revd Canon Charles Patteson 'for so long as he remains the Vicar of that Parish' and Sydney David McCloy 'for life', the Coöptative Trustees could be reappointed. They were to hold at least two meetings a year, three people constituted a quorum, the Chairman was to have a casting vote, minutes and accounts were to be kept as required by the Charity Commissioners and the Trustees could 'appoint some fit person to be their Clerk.'

The Charity was designed to benefit:

'friendless boys and girls who are under the age of 18 years and who are in need of assistance to enable them to be maintained, clothed and educated. Any boy or girl may be deemed to be friendless if he or she has no parent or other relative or guardian upon whom he or she can rely for the ordinary necessities of life.'

Its purpose was to maintain, clothe and educate qualified beneficiaries in such a manner as the Trustees think fit:

'education at a school maintained or supported by a Local Education Authority ... or on a Training Ship or at a Sea Training School, and to attendance at night classes or other classes for instruction in technical subjects.'

It also gives the Trustees permission to use the income as *'subscriptions or donations to any Home, Society or Institution in or in the neighbourhood of Scarborough'* with similar objectives.

They could give a grant for a child to be accommodated in a Home; supply *'clothing, boots or linen either by means of money grants or in kind';* assist toward other than elementary education and provide outfits, pay fees or travelling expenses for those who were taking up any trade or occupation. It particularly mentions that the Charity *'shall not be applied in any case in aid of any rates.'*

From the list of eight existing beneficiaries the fee of £17 10s was paid to the Convent of Mary on behalf of Violet Mary Agar; £3 15s 5d went to J G Holroyd for his College expenses; £40 was paid to Mr Howard of the Boys' High School in respect of Denis Rogers. The highest amount given was £75 to Arthur Bastow for his fees and expenses at University College, Nottingham while Revd J R Trotter was advanced £33 13s 4d for Denis Rogers at the High School. Maintenance grants were given, £10 for Eric Newham, £10 for Audrey Swift, £3 4s for Peter Judson and £3 8s for Denis Crabtree.

The Charity held three freehold properties, 'Wedgewood Court' Deepdale, £2,550 at 5% interest; 20 Prince of Wales Terrace, a boarding house, £1,500 at 4% interest and 15 and 15A North Street, £3,200 also at 4% interest. Various amounts of War Stock and Savings Bonds totalling £10,991 5s 4d were held in the names of various people including Revd Percy Reginald Watts, Henry Edward Donner (deceased), Revd Charles Patteson, Revd James Ridley Trotter and Sydney David McCloy.

The first three meetings in February 1942 were held at the Vicarage. Canon Patteson and Mr McCloy saw that the Scheme was correctly administered: Revd J R Trotter of All Saints Church and Miss Frances Mary Spofforth of 15 Avenue Victoria were appointed Coöptative Trustees: Mr McCloy, Miss Spofforth and Mr John S Stephenson of 7 Cromwell Road were appointed Investment Trustees. The four meetings a year were to be held at the 'Alice Brooke' Home, 6 Belgrave Crescent and Mr Arthur Steele, also of 38 Queen Street, was to be the Clerk at a salary of £10 per annum in addition to expenses. The Westminster Bank

Limited was selected and their deeds and securities were to be deposited there.

At 3 o'clock on 1 May 1942, The Mayor, Councillor J C Ireland; Alderman J W Butler of 8 Seamer Road, appointed by the Local Education Authority; Revd P R Watts of St Thomas' Vicarage in Longwestgate; Revd J R Trotter, Vicar of All Saints, 2 Westover Road; Miss F M Spofforth and Mr S D McCloy met in the Alice Brooke Home. There were two main items for discussion: Violet Mary Agar, who had been admitted as a boarder at the Convent of the Ladies of Mary, had been taken ill with rheumatic fever and had to be sent home to Hull by ambulance so would not be able to sit for her School Certificate Examination: they decided to allow Convent to keep the cheque. The second concerned Minnie Devonshire, a widow living in Maple Drive, who had requested a grant towards the cost of the initial outfit for her son, William, to enter the Merchant Service as an apprentice in August. In view of the good report from the Headmaster at the Graham Sea Training School, this was granted: the country was half-way through the Second World War.

The Earlier years

There is evidence that the charity had been operating since the legacy had been received, long before it came under the Charity Commissioners. The Education Committee Meeting held on 21 July 1925 with Alderman Ascough in the Chair and Councillor Butler attending, recorded a letter from Mr H E Donner to the effect:

> *The Trustees of the John Kendall Trust had agreed to make the following grants to the Conway and the Graham Sea Training Scholarship winners:-*
> *(1) £50 a year for 2 years to Leslie Burkill*
> *(2) A sum of £10 to each of the following:-*
> *(a) Lawrence Binns*

    (b) Richard Russell
    (c) Kenneth Swales
    (d) Benjamin Hanson
    (e) Albert Macdonald

The Secretary was instructed to convey thanks to the John Kendall Trust. There was a follow-up in the Minutes of 28 September 1925, we read:

'letter of 16 September re payment of Scholarship money promised by the John Kendall Trust.
Resolved: That the Education Committee recommend the scholarship provided by the John Kendall Trust be paid in three equal instalments in October, January and July.'

The John Kendall Trust was also known to the Amicable Society as their minutes of 27 November 1931 tell of a letter sent from Lieut. H H Heather, Headmaster of Graham Sea Training School requesting assistance for Harry Moon of 2 Hope's Yard, Longwestgate to remain in the school to the age of sixteen and then proceed to sea. They resolved that if Mr J Jackson made a satisfactory report, the case would be referred to Mr H E Donner so that an application could be made either to the John Kendall Trust or the Scarborough United Scholarships Foundation. It was resolved at the next meeting that no further action be taken in this case and his brother William's application for boots was turned down too.

    We should look at the Solicitors who were already running the trust. Henry Donner was born in 1859, he was a solicitor with McCloy in Queen Street whom we have already met in connection with the other charities. His forebears go back to the old Common Hall; in 1832 Edward Donner was one of the Bailiffs while his son Edward Sedgefield Donner, Henry's father, was a Coroner. Grandfather Edward ran the Assembly Room at 25 Longroom Street which was used by the Corporation after their move from Sandside. In 1840 Edward Sedgefield is listed in the directory as being a solicitor with Woodalls and Clerk to both the Magistrates and the Board of Guardians. He was also named as the Corporation Solicitor in the Bleach House Trial of 1833. Our Trustee Henry married Emily in 1901 and was living in Cloughton, they had no children; in 1924 he bought a house in the Crescent. He died in 1939 and his house was acquired by the Council in 1942, we now know it as the Art Gallery.

Sydney McCloy, born in the Barnsley area in 1904, was also working with the solicitors Watts, Kitching, Donner and McCloy. He married Doris Whitworth in 1935 in Scarborough and lived to the grand age of 96. Watts and Kitching were listed as solicitors in Bulmer's Directory of 1890 in their premises at 38 Queen Street. The firm remained at 37 and 38 Queen Street until 1972 when it moved to 18 Queen Street. Arthur Steele was a clerk in the firm as well as being clerk to the Trust. After he retired the cashier, Ronnie Carr, continued to deal with the Charity's administration, including the preparation of the annual accounts.

The firm subsequently amalgamated with Bedwell's and moved to their premises at 32 Queen Street. Mr McCloy was godfather to Hilary Watts who still works in this firm of solicitors, his father having joined them in 1940. We find a further connection in that Hilary's grandfather was Revd P R Watts, Vicar of St Thomas' Church on Sandside. He has already been mentioned as holding War Stock and Savings Bonds in the Trust's original document and as a member of the first John Kendall Trust committee of 1941. It would seem logical, in the absence of Revd Charles Swinnerton, for his successor as Vicar of St Thomas' Church to take on this role. Canon Patteson and Revd Watts were also Governors of SUSF, then, in 1940 Sydney McCloy took over as its Secretary on the death of Mr Donner so the charities were already interlinked.

In addition to the grants mentioned, it would appear that the John Kendall Trust had an historical affiliation to the Alice Brooke Home, Scarborough's home for friendless girls as that is where the Trustees met from 1 May 1942 until 15 January 1963.

The Alice Brooke Home

Currently part of Normanby House Residential Home, number 6 Belgrave Crescent, is where the Alice Brooke Home for Girls used to be. It was established through the Church of England Homes for Waifs and Strays, later to become the Church of England Children's Society, now it is known simply as the Children's Society. The opening ceremony was performed on 7 October 1912 by Revd H F E Wigram, Vicar of St Thomas' Church from 1911 to 1918, and the newly appointed Bishop of Hull, Rt Revd J A Kempthorne. Money had been donated by Mr and Miss Brooke, initially to enable girls from Scarborough to be accommodated in other homes. It was considered preferable for the girls to remain in Scarborough so Mr and Mrs J W Drew helped to fund the purchase of this house which had room for 25 girls aged between 3 and 16 years.

Who then was Alice Brooke? From digging in the Genealogist records I have found a Lithographer, William Brooke who was born in York in 1836, his father had been a farmer in Basingstoke, Hampshire. In the 1861 census William and his family, including his father, Benjamin, were living at 12 New Queen Street. His wife, Fanny (née Pearson) came from Leeds and already had a son, Charles, from her previous marriage to Charles Guest.

They had moved to 4 Hyde Park Terrace on Victoria Road in the 1871 census where they were employing a man and four boys. By 1881 they were at 1 West Grove Terrace, Falsgrave, the far end of the terrace where the Ascoughs were living; this time William's occupation is given as 'Stationer etc.' In both the 1901 and the 1911 records, William was living at 120 Falsgrave Road which was the same house but it now came under Scarborough's addressing system. William was still a lithographer and engraver at the age of 75, his wife Fanny had died in 1888. William reached the age of 86, he died in York in 1922.

William and Fanny had six children, Sydney was born in 1862 and followed his father as a lithographer, he was living at home on the 1901 census. Ada was born in 1864 and Maria, later known as Mary Louise, arrived in 1865. She was the only one living at home on the 1911 census and so must have been the Miss Brooke who donated the money with her father. Mary lived to the age of 92 and died in Scarborough in 1958. There were two more boys, William born in 1868 and Benjamin the following year. Benjamin married a Scarborough girl, Charlotte, became a Chemist and Druggist and moved to Gillygate, in York so his father may have been living there when he died. There is a birth record of Alice in 1870 but she does not appear on any census so we may assume that The Alice Brooke Home was named in her memory.

A Winter postcard 1919. Alice Brooke Home for Girls.

A photograph dated 1919, shows a snowy scene, possibly taken at Christmas, with 25 children ranged on the steps outside the home and three members of staff, one is named as the Matron, Miss Ann Hool. By this time the Waifs and Strays, which had been started in 1882 in Dulwich, cared for five thousand children in its 113 homes. During the First World War the children from the Alice Brooke Home were moved to Snainton, some ten miles away but returned to Belgrave Square where they remained until 1963.

It is reported that from the 1920s, the girls were members of the Girl Guide Movement and earned their badges by doing jobs around the house. This was one of the last homes to remain 'girls only'. In 1969, six years after their move to a converted farmhouse on Scalby Road named Danes Dyke, boys from the Waterloo Children's Society Home in Lancashire, Elm Lodge, joined them together with their house parents, Mr and Mrs Hamer. The Children's Society changed its policy to adoption and fostering rather than providing residential homes; they also began working with the youth justice sector so the home on Scalby Road was closed in 1971.

Scarborough Amicable Society's Balance Sheet for the year ending 31 March 1984, records the receipt of £5,000 from the Alice Brooke Fund. We can assume that the house was sold and this was the charity chosen to benefit. The Officers at the time were Mr N Waller, Treasurer, Mr F Green and Miss B W Clayton, joint Secretaries and Mr John D Morley President.

From 1980

After the closure of the Alice Brooke Home in Belgrave Square, The John Kendall Trust met less regularly. With Revd J Keys Fraser newly installed as Vicar of Scarborough in 1964, their meetings were again held in the Vicarage but there was a gap from March 1972 to July 1980. Mr McCloy continued to see that grants were paid to the children in their new quarters, mainly into the Clothing Fund, as well as to other applicants. It had been suggested that Mr McCloy should enquire of the Charity Commissioners the future use of the funds as there were very few applications.

When Councillor H R Bedford was elected Mayor in 1980, things began to change. He had been on the Amicable Society Committee since 30 June 1949 and was one of their six representatives on the SUSF, appointed on 8 May 1958, so he was well aware of the work of the children's charities. Bob, as he was always known, had been born in Leeds but came to teach in Scarborough at St Mary's Junior Mixed School in the 1930s. After returning from service as a Flying Officer in the RAF during the Second World War, he taught at Central School. His first headship was at Overdale Primary School then he moved to Gladstone Road Juniors, retiring in 1980. He had been elected to the Borough Council in 1969.

Councillor H R Bedford took the Chair at the meeting in the Vicarage on 29 July 1980. Also present were Mr S D McCloy, Mrs M L Priestly, as representative trustee from the Local Education Authority and the Revd Frank Mitchell, Vicar of St Saviour's with All Saints representing the Ecclesiastical Parishes. The meeting then elected three Coöptative Trustees, Canon J Keys Fraser, Miss L A Drew MBE and Mr P A Gardiner, Headmaster of the Boys' High School. It is interesting to note that Miss Lorna A Drew had first signed the book as a Trustee of the charity on 9 May 1947 and Mrs Mary Priestley on 6 June 1967. Perhaps the fact that both were also on the SUSF Committee, appointed by the Scarborough Divisional Executive since 21 April 1948 had some bearing. Mr Gardiner had joined the John Kendall Trust on 8 December 1970.

The meeting on 29 July reconvened with the full complement of seven trustees and Revd Keys Fraser was elected Chairman. The Income and Expenditure Accounts for the period 1 January 1972 to 30 June 1980 were presented and approved and the purpose of the gathering 'Winding up of the Trust and Distribution of the Funds' was discussed. The winding up was not in doubt: the funds would be distributed by giving £5,000 to the Church of England Children's Society and the balance would be donated to the National Children's Home, the Methodist equivalent, May Lodge. This home for boys had been set up on Filey Road in 1966, it is now converted into flats but still bears the name. The service for families with children with disabilities was moved to Cherry Drive and continues under the name of May Lodge.

It would appear that the Charity Commissioners refused to allow the John Kendall Trust to wind up. At the Trustees' meeting on 30 September 1980 they resolved to donate £8,000 from previous years' income plus £750 from the current year to the National Children's Home for its work at May Lodge in Filey Road. They would invest the rest of the money in a charitable fund and hold meetings of the charity twice a year. The Clerk, Mr A H Carr, would write to the Rural Dean, the Scarborough Area Education Officer, the Scarborough Social Services Officer, the Senior Probation Officer for Scarborough and the Secretary of the Scarborough Amicable Society to invite *'names and particulars of any Qualified Beneficiaries known to them for consideration'*. Mr Carr's salary was £200 for his services to date.

At their meeting in April 1981, they agreed to write to the Heads of all the schools for suitable beneficiaries. Various recommendations suggested by the Charity Commissioners to the Scheme were implemented and the venue for future meetings was to be the Town Hall, through the good offices of Councillor Bedford. He completed his two years as Mayor and was made a trustee again in 1984, representing the County Council Education Committee when Mrs Priestley stood down.

The John Kendall Trust continued, mainly supporting May Lodge but they also found two children from Scarborough who were being cared for through the Children's Society whom they supported to the age of 18. Occasionally a grant towards clothing was given to a local pupil. A plaque 9" by 12" was commissioned from Mr Peter Blades to be installed in May Lodge with the words

'In memory of Col John Kendall, who died on 21 February 1923, Benefactor of the Children of Scarborough.'

The Minutes of 5 October 1984 report that the plaque had been installed; the Trustees arranged to inspect it at 3.30 pm on 7 May 1985.

The Charity's final resolution was made on 15 April 1988 when it resolved to apply to the Charity Commissioners to:

'make a Scheme appointing the Governors for the time being of the Scarborough United Scholarships Foundation to be the Trustees of the John Kendall Trust.'

The decision was made by Canon J Keys Fraser, S D McCloy, Councillor H R Bedford and Mrs Shirley Gorton, Headmistress of Gladstone Road Infants School. Fittingly it was to be signed by Canon John Keys Fraser, Vicar of Scarborough and Mr Sydney McCloy, who had served the charity faithfully for all its 47 years and possibly more. Equally fittingly, Councillor H R Bedford was the Chairman of the partner, the SUSF, and remained so until he resigned on 19 January 2007. He died in 2012 having given service over a period of 58 years to the three Scarborough Children's Charities.

Colonel John Kendall

Of the benefactor, John Kendall, little was known. Through various means, mainly via Google, I have discovered that he was the son of Revd Frederick Kendall, Vicar of Riccall and his wife Frances, née Hobson, of Sheepscar Lodge, Leeds, now in Leeds city centre. He was born in York in 1830 although he also gives Skipton as his place of birth. His mother had been born in 1811, the daughter of Richard Hobson, a practicing physician of Queen's College, Cambridge, and his wife, Caroline, they had connections in Leeds and York. I was able to find details of his military career but you will understand why his childhood was difficult to trace later in the chapter.

John Kendall enlisted in 3rd Regiment of West York Militia around 1852 when Queen Victoria decreed it should be a Light Infantry Corps. They did their training in Doncaster for 28 days in May 1854 then proceeded to Berwick. The men were supplied with their uniforms, two shirts, two pairs of half stockings and boots plus a suit consisting of coatee and trousers, with lace decoration in silver rather than gold. Sergeants were given two pairs of boots while other ranks only got one pair per annum; after a year the uniform became the man's property. The details come from George Alfred Raikes in his book on the history of this regiment.

On 21 June the Regiment left Berwick for Dublin, the soldiers were asked to serve abroad but those who did not wish to were allowed to go home. In May 1855 the regiment moved from Dublin to Waterford where they were presented with new colours, the daughter of Colonel Ferrars Loftus performed the honours. At this time the country was fighting in the Crimean War with the Turkish contingent against the Russians. And John Kendall's Regiment? They moved to Belfast where there was a mêlée with some civilians on the quayside as they embarked on 29 May 1856 on their way to Fleetwood.

In 1856 their regiment was disembodied. Some regiments were being sent to India but our 3rd Regiment of West Yorks Militia was called to Doncaster in September 1857. They travelled to Aldershot by rail on 11 November. In 1858 the Brown Bess muskets were replaced by Enfield rifles and their regimental badge, the white rose of York which had originally been conferred in 1811 was approved by Queen Victoria on 15 August 1860.

During this period the soldiers were deployed in various northern towns, Newcastle, Sunderland and Carlisle. They continued to train for some 28 days each year in Doncaster. John Kendall had risen from being a lieutenant in 1852 to captain the following year and major in 1870. On 30 July 1873 John Kendall was made an Honorary Lieutenant Colonel in the 3rd Regiment of the West York Militia. Such was the military career of Colonel John Kendall.

As for his family life: in the Leeds Mercury of 24 April 1864 we read:

'on 20 April 1864 John Kendall Esq. of Skipton-on-Swale, son of the late Rev Frederick Kendall of Riccall, married Caroline Althea Woodall, only daughter of W E Woodall in St Mary's Church, Scarborough, the Revd Dr Whiteside officiated'.

Caroline Althea had been on the Ladies Committee of the Amicable Society in 1862 while her father was a member of their Musical Committee. John and Caroline had one son, John Frederick William Kendall, born in Skipton in 1866. They moved to Scarborough and on the 1871 census, John Kendall, County Magistrate, together with his family, were living at 3 Gordon House on West Street. They were still living at this address on the 1911 census. Incidentally this is next-door to where Charlotte Morley was living in 1871 so perhaps they had known each other when Caroline was on the Ladies' Committee of the Amicable Society before her marriage.

Young John went to Rugby School, he appears on the 1881 census in a school boarding house on Barby Road. Philip Bowden-Smith, Professor of Modern Languages and his family were in residence: the Headmaster at the time was Thomas Jex-Blake. H S Torrens informs us that John matriculated at Hertford College, Oxford in 1885 but there is no further information about him, not even a record of his death. Caroline Althea died towards the end of 1911.

The minutes of the Scarborough School Board record that Colonel Kendall was elected to that committee following the resignation of the Revd R Brown-Borthwick, Vicar of All Saints' Church in Falsgrave. Meredith Whittaker was the Chairman at the time, the Vice Chairman was John Rowntree and other members included Miss Florence Balgarnie, Revd Dolan, Revd Parr, Mr A Kitson and Mr G S Welburn. His first meeting was on 13 October 1884; he attended regularly but did not stand for election in 1886.

On 1 February 1896, Colonel Kendall endowed eight almshouses in St Mary's Street with £2,074 South Eastern Railway stock, this was sufficient to keep them maintained. Reference to Col John Kendall's library appears in the Education Committee Minutes of 12 November 1923 when it was resolved:

'the question of storage of the above library pending the provision of a suitable building be left in the hands of the Chairman (Councillor Anderson) Secretary Mr D W Buron and the Head Master of the Scarborough Boys' High School.'

There is no record in the minutes as to what happened to the books but part of the collection went to the Scarborough Library. We may assume that this branch of the family had died out and John Kendall wished to dispose of his assets to benefit the town of Scarborough.

While John Kendall was on the School Board, William Ascough gave a particularly vehement account of the problems affecting school attendance. The Report on the Working of the Bye Laws Committee in 1884 was printed in the local paper and pasted into the minutes of 15 December 1884. As a requirement of the Education Acts and the Bye Laws of the School Board, they had to account for any children who were not attending school regularly or who were found wandering the streets. If the pupils' attendance did not improve the families were summoned before the magistrates. During that year the Attendance Officers had held 7,550 special inquiries and paid 941 visits to serve notice on negligent parents. The Bye Laws Committee had met 38 times and heard 893 cases of which 111 were sent to court. William Ascough instanced six cases:

1. A child of 8 not attending school, Mother states no clothes, father drinks, Mother drinks, the child is locked up in the house. Mother promises to do better.
2. Husband at work, mother at laundry, three children 9, 5, 3 locked in the house.
3. Widow leaves home for work at 7 am, children aged 8 and 6 left in the house, they stay in bed and remain at home all day.
4. Father, bricklayer has no work, walks to Sheffield. Mother is charring to keep herself and six children, eldest child, girl of 11, stays at home to look after baby.
5. Fisherman not able to work due to rheumatism, Mother goes out washing, four children, eldest girl aged 12 looks after the 12 month old baby.
6. Husband deserted wife who works in the Fish-house and other places to keep herself and three children, eldest aged 8 looks after 2 year old.

He also recalled a speech made by Mr Mundella who had spoken to the Director of schools in Canton Lucerne, Switzerland where the children of the poor throughout the country were provided for by a voluntary society. He thought the teachers in the elementary schools in Scarborough would welcome this. Attendance had gone up to 80 per cent on average, although the figures had been affected by a bad epidemic of measles since September.

Could this, together with his experience as a magistrate, have moved John Kendall to create the trust to help similar *'friendless boys and girls'*?

The Woodalls of Scarborough

John Kendall's wife, Caroline Althea Woodall, had been born into Scarborough's ruling dynasty that was the Woodall family. Although we are told there were members of the Woodall family in the Common Hall in 16th century, in Hinderwell's list of Scarborough Bailiffs his first recorded Woodall is John, a Junior Bailiff in 1789. In 1745 John had married Elizabeth and two years later we find he was master of a ship called 'Unanimity'; their son John was, born in 1747 too. Father John became a Senior Bailiff in 1792 and his son, John Woodall junior, was a Junior Bailiff in 1804; they were joined in 1827 by John Woodall, tertious, as a Junior Bailiff. We have already seen that the Woodall family had been great supporters of the Amicable Society over many years.

G Broadrick published a 'New Scarborough Guide' in 1811 and kindly lists the members of the Common Hall. The First Twelve are named as: Mr James Tindall, Mr Thomas Hinderwell, Mr John Woodall Sen., Mr Thomas Foster, Mr Valentine Fowler, Mr John Coulson, Mr Benjamin Fowler, Mr Anthony Beswick, Mr John Travis, Mr Gawan Taylor, Mr William Travis and Mr John Woodall Jun.; the Recorder was the Duke of Rutland (various Dukes of Rutland sat as MP for Scarborough) and Mr John Travis was the Deputy Recorder and Common Clerk. The Representatives in Parliament at the time were the Hon. Lieutenant-General Phipps and the Rt. Hon. Charles Manners Sutton, who was connected to the Duke of Rutland and became a member of the Privy Council.

Around 1835, just before the new Borough Council legislation came into being, Robert Hornsey, a 'Schoolmaster and private teacher of the English and French Languages' had his 'Visitant's Guide' printed by C R Todd. In it he also lists the Bailiffs, obviously essential tourist information. His Grace the Duke of Rutland continued as Recorder but Mr John Woodall became the Common Clerk as well as being in the First Twelve. Mr William E Woodall was Chamberlain and they were joined by two more family members, his brothers Thomas and Henry Woodall. Included in the vast amount of information we find Revd H R Millar was Vicar of St Mary's, Revd Robert Howard, Vicar of Christ Church and John Mitchell, Master and Ann Marshall, Mistress at the Amicable School.

The Woodalls bought up land and were involved with many enterprises in the town. The building of a bridge to enable the season's visitors access the Spa was a great undertaking; we have already heard that the charities had investments in the Scarborough Cliff Bridge Company. It is no surprise then to find some familiar names among the members of the Company. E H Hebden Esq. Senior Bailiff and banker with John Woodall, laid the first stone, in the presence of the junior Bailiff, Mr George Nesfield on 29 November 1826, in the reign of George lV. John Woodall was the Treasurer and Sir George Cayley was one of the three trustees. William Travis was on the Management Committee, which had five members from Scarborough and six from York. It was built by Messrs Stead, Snowdon and Buckley, Contractors of York with John Outhet as the engineer.

Thomas Hinderwell describes the opening of the bridge on 19 July 1827:

'The day was unusually fine, the sky was unclouded, and scarcely a breeze played upon the bosom of the mighty ocean. ... At five o'clock about eighty people sat

down to a sumptuous and elegant dinner, at Donner's Hotel'

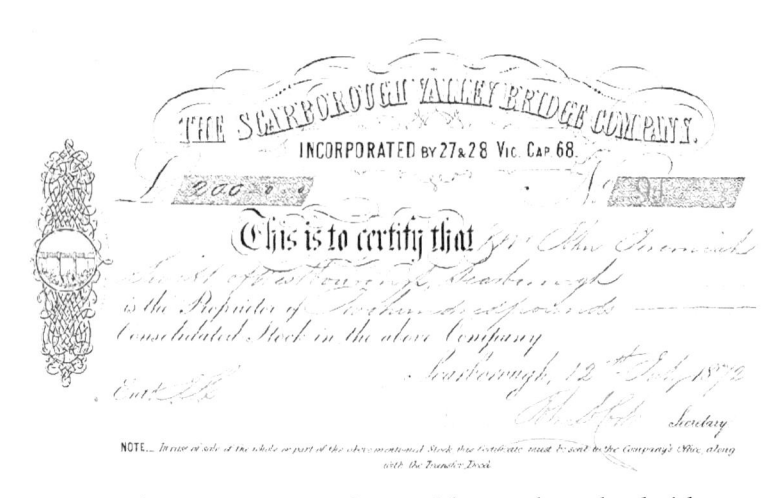

[Scarborough Valley Bridge Company share certificate]

In order to reassure the residents that the bridge was safe, bankers Hebden and Woodall riding in a horse-drawn stage coach were among the first to cross. The bridge provided a perfect promenade for the gentry; it was 350 yards long and cost over £9,000 to build. The funds were raised initially by selling six hundred shares at £10 each. As Hinderwell put it from the viewpoint of the Georgian society of his day:

'It affords a walk from which improper classes are excluded.'

This was the same bridge the children from the Amicable Schools marched across to their Celebration Day picnic in 1860.

Hebden and Woodall were involved in another business venture in 1866, the building of the North Bay pier at a cost of £12,135. This was before the Marine Drive was built and did not prove to be a very successful venture; it was destroyed by a tremendous gale in 1905. Their original bank was on Palace Hill, the lower end of Eastborough, before it moved into premises in Queen Street where Boyes'

Store now stands. By 1840 the partners also included John Tindall, John Cocks and John Woodall junior. They moved to the corner of St Nicholas Street and in 1896 it amalgamated with Barclay's Bank which is still in the same premises.

The John Woodall who was born in 1747, had started the bank, he lived at 22 Long Room Street. He and his wife, Ann, had four sons; John, the banker, born in 1801; Henry born in 1806; Thomas Dowker born 1807 and William Edward, born in 1809. Father John died in 1835 and in the 1841 census his widow was living in Princess Street while William and Henry were living in the family house on St Nicholas Cliff.

William had married Caroline Althea from Gainsborough in Lincolnshire. They had two children, Caroline Althea who became John Kendall's wife, was born in 1836 and William Otter was born the following year. Brother Henry had married Maria Elizabeth from Scarborough and their daughter, Mary Elizabeth, was born in 1835. Also living in the house we find two male servants and four female servants.

The other brother, Thomas, married Sarah Pitt in Leyton, he became a Magistrate in 1832 but then left Scarborough due to ill health. He died aged 32, on 2 January 1839; his son, Thomas, born in 1828, later became a Major in the army.

John the banker who had been living in Belvoir Terrace, inherited his father's house, had it demolished and built the mansion, St Nicholas House, in 1846. It is this Jacobean style brick building, designed by Henry Wyatt that forms the greater part of the present Town Hall. John married Mary Eleanor from Grantham in Lincolnshire and had six children. John Woodall was born in 1832, Charles in 1833, Mary Hebden in 1835, Louisa in 1836, Edith in 1839, Edward Henry in 1843 and finally Augusta in 1845.

Mary married John Dent Dent of Ribstone Hall in 1855, he had been a captain of the Yorkshire Hussars. He became MP for Scarborough from 1857 to 1874, they had six children, their eldest daughter was Mary Catherine who served on the Board of Education in 1901. Louisa married in 1876 she became the second wife of Revd Arthur William Headlam, Vicar of St Oswald's Church in Durham, but did not have any children. Her husband already had three sons and a daughter, the eldest son, Arthur Cayley Headlam became the Principal of Kings College London.

John Woodall Woodall was educated at Rugby and studied Natural Sciences at Oriel College, Oxford. He joined the family bank and also took a great interest in the fishing industry and the study of fish to the extent that he made plans to develop fish farming in the area because he noticed the stocks were dwindling. 'The Garland' was his specially designed yacht, he used it to carry out research in the North Sea and the Humber Estuary. According to the interview he gave for 'The Scarborough Magazine' re-printed as 'Some Scarborough Faces, past and present' in 1901, he gave evidence to royal commissions and spoke at international conferences on the subject.

He had an exhibition hall built on Foreshore Road that seated five thousand people; it became The Olympia but was burnt down in 1975. John W had 'well-appointed workshops' in the grounds of St Nicholas House where he *'designed and built vessels, refitted his yachts, made handsome cabinet work, etc.'* At the time he was making an octagonal table with a five pointed star representing the five continents and inlaid with over fifty rare woods. He had even laid the floor in the 'handsome drawing room' with oak and canary pine.

The Maritime Heritage Museum tells us that John Woodall Woodall served in the Militia during the Crimean War from 1853 to 56. The 'New Army List' dated 1 July 1867 records him being promoted to major on 12 May 1866 in the East and North York Artillery, whose headquarters was at Scarborough. John W was elected to the borough council in 1863 and served three times as Mayor, 1868, 1881 and

1886. He inherited the house in 1879 on the death of his father, who had also served as Mayor in 1851. John W retained his seat as councillor and later was made an Alderman until he retired in 1889. The 'Scarborough Faces' article tells us that John W remained 'true to his old leader' in the Liberal Association even though his brother Charles became a prominent Unionist. He also mentions that brother Edward was *'the reigning genius in the agricultural or horticultural departments'*.

John W was a very prominent member of the Freemasons; he was elected Grand Treasurer in 1885 and he moved to London. During his time in Scarborough he held a number of public positions: he was a Justice of the Peace, a Deputy-Lieutenant for the North Riding, a member of the North Riding County Council, Chairman of the Harbour Trust, an Hon. Lieutenant of the Royal Naval Reserve and a director of the Electric Supply Company. When he sold the estate in 1898, the borough council bought the house, extended it and opened it as the Town Hall in 1903. Jack Binns tells us that the Woodall family owned the greater part of the land in the north of Scarborough up to Peasholm Beck.

In the 1881 census brothers John Woodall, Charles William and Edward Henry together with sisters, Edith and Augusta, were all living with their 72 year old mother, Mary Eleanor, in St Nicholas House. Their ten servants comprised a cook, two lady's maids, an upper housemaid, a kitchen maid, an under housemaid and a scullery maid with a butler, a footman and a groom. In the 1891 census, Henry is the only one recorded as still living in the house.

John Woodall Woodall's brother, William Edward, Caroline Althea's father, had moved his family to 4 Belmont Terrace on the 1851 census with just a lady's maid in residence. William was by now an Attorney and Solicitor; he later added the role of Registrar. By 1861 they were at 11 The Crescent with a cook, a house maid, a kitchen maid and a lady's maid, Josephine Le Couttie, from Morges in Switzerland.

Young Caroline Althea married John Kendall in 1864: when they came to live in Scarborough the 1871 census records them having a cook, a house maid, a parlour maid and a kitchen maid. Her mother, Caroline Althea, died in 1867. William Edward Woodall and his son, William Otter, continued to live in the Crescent until 1891. William Edward remarried, and in the 1891 census he and his wife, Ann, were living in Westbourne Road.

Caroline's brother, William Otter Woodall, had been educated at King's School, Canterbury; he lived in St Giles, Finsbury, London before marrying Mary Candler from Monk Fryston in 1863. Their son, William Candler Woodall, was born in 1863. On the 1881 census William and Mary Woodall are listed among the guests in the Grand Hotel. William Candler followed his father's profession as an Attorney and Registrar in Scarborough, he was in business with Bedwells at 32 Queen Street. We have now come full circle as this is the firm Sydney McCloy joined.

Reverend Frederick Kendall

If John Kendall does not appear to have had a particularly illustrious career, perhaps we should take a look at his father. Frederick Kendall was born on 1 September 1790 in the small village of Nunnington not far from Helmsley, to Rear Admiral John Kendall and his wife, Ann. From the church records we find he was baptised at the church in the nearby village of Stonegrave on 4 September 1790. A memorial plaque was erected in this church after his death in 1836 when his son John was only 6 years old.

The 'Alumni Cantabrigienses' edited by John Venn, informs us that Frederick went to Mr Richardson's school in Malton before going to Mr Huggitt in Denham (or could that be Durham?) and thence to Trinity College Cambridge. He matriculated in 1809 but 'migrated' to

Sidney College on 13 June 1810 and gained his BA in 1813. Apparently he was dissatisfied with his marks and when three fires were discovered in the college, suspicion fell on Frederick. At this time arson was a capital offence and Frederick was described as a very highly strung student and 'heir to a considerable fortune'. His father hired the services of the Solicitor General, William Garrow, who had the case quickly dismissed based on the fact that the illiterate watchman on duty could not read the evidence he had given verbally.

Frederick Kendall returned to his father's house in Auborough Street, Scarborough, where he worked on his fossil collection. This was not a mere hobby, Frederick had scoured the area coastal-wise from Hornsea to Mulgrave and inland to Malton; his 'Catalogue' which is over 300 pages long records the location of different minerals and different types of fossils, its full title is *A Descriptive Catalogue of the Minerals and Fossil Organic Remains of Scarborough and the Vicinity'*. Each entry is beautifully described and there are some exquisite illustrations, probably the work of James Sowerby.

The Catalogue was printed in Scarborough by Thomas Coultas in 1816. Its long list of subscribers includes many familiar names including: William Bean; Henry Byron; Sir George Cayley; Constable of Burton Constable; Thomas Hinderwell; E H Hebden; William Harland; Thomas Harland; Earl of Mulgrave; Rt. Hon. Lord Normanby; Rt Hon General Phipps; The Corporation Scarborough; Sir M M Sykes, Sledmere; Revd Sykes, Westow; John Tindall, Scarborough; Miss Mary Tindall; Revd James Tindall, Leicestershire; John Tindall, West Gate, Scarborough; William Travis; John Woodall, Scarborough; John Woodall, jun. Scarborough; William Worsley Esq., Stonegrave.

Amongst the sites Frederick visited are limestone quarries at Flamborough, Ayton, Ebberston, Pickering and Malton. He found alum at Peake, better known as Robin Hood's Bay, and Stowbrow; at Hinderskelf Park, that is

Castle Howard, he discovered shark teeth and elephant teeth at Whitby. He found oyster shell fossils in

'a part of the slaty cliffs near the Spaw at Scarborough which shot down a few years ago.'

He does not give an exact location for the amethyst, garnet and beryl he found but *'for a considerable extent along the shore'* he came across carnelian. He gives a charming description of finding jade in a chalk cliff:

'leek green passing to greenish white. Translucent, feels greasy... sometimes has a glimmering silky lustre.'

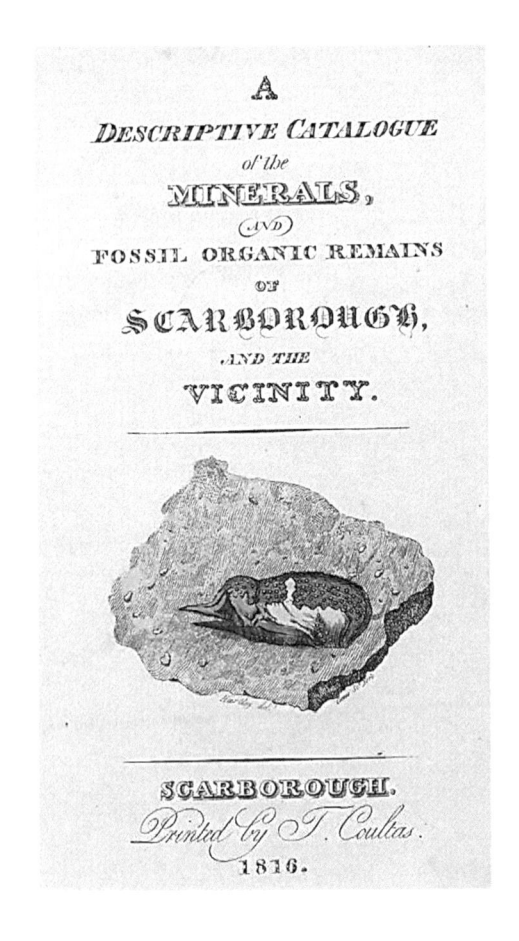

From Mr Charlton's 'History of Whitby' he recalls that in 1743 Revd Mr Borwick found the complete skeleton or petrified bones of a man, unfortunately it broke up during the excavation. A fossilised crocodile was also found under the cliff and the alum works at Saltwick revealed the fossilised bones of a horse.

Frederick was not the only collector of fossils, William Bean is said to have had the country's most important fossil collection, he was also a keen naturalist and collector of shells. William's grandfather was a market gardener in Brompton in the 1700s: his father, William, moved to Scarborough and created a pleasure garden around 1790 to the south of Huntriss Row. William was born in 1787 at 6 Vernon Place, he sold his father's garden possibly to finance his fossil collection. On the 1861 census he is described as being Independent and an Alderman. This would have been the gentleman who was a Grammar School Trustee when the field was sold to the Railway Company. His son, William, was born in 1816 and became a botanist.

Another fossil collector was Thomas Hinderwell the Historian and early member of the Amicable Society. He also had a large collection of books and manuscripts according to Peter C Robinson in his article 'Early Scarborough Geologists'. It was hardly surprising that the renowned geologist, William Smith, was attracted to the area, he accepted a post as land steward at Hackness for four years from 1824 with Sir John Bempde Johnstone, father of Sir Harcourt Johnstone.

Mr Robinson tells us that Dr John Dunn, medical partner to Dr William Travis who too was a keen botanist, hosted a meeting with these gentlemen in 1820. Together with support from Sir George Cayley and Frances Richardson Currer of Skipton, who had inherited a vast collection of prints, shells and fossils from her great grandfather, they made plans to set up the Rotunda Museum. Stone was provided from the Johnstone's quarry at Hackness, expertise from William Smith's nephew, John

Phillips, and the domed building was opened as the Rotunda Museum in 1830.

Meanwhile Frederick Kendall found a post as Curate to Thomas Gilbart at Burton Fleming in 1816 and became a priest the next year on the same stipend of £40. In 1818 he moved as Vicar to the ancient Parish Church of St Mary in Riccall near York where he remained until his death in 1836. It is recorded in the Hull Advertiser and Exchange Gazette of 24 September 1824 that Frederick officiated at the wedding at Riccall of Samuel Standidge Byron of Scarborough to Sophia, the daughter of the late Edward Lowe of Galway, granddaughter of the late Admiral Kendall of Scarborough. Sophia would have been Frederick's niece. Sadly, the Leeds Intelligence of 7 October graphically reported the death of Sophia at Boroughbridge:

> *'A most melancholy instance of the uncertainty of human life, and the instability of sublunary bliss, occurred at Boroughbridge, on Tuesday week, in the sudden death of Mrs. Byron, in the 18th year of her age... Her marriage took place on the 23rd ult., and she was a corpse on the 28th'.*

This was the same Samuel Byron who cross-examined the local worthies over Bleach House in 1833. Samuel married again, he and Elizabeth had two children, Thomas and Agnes.

Frederick's marriage to Frances Hobson in 1826 produced two sons. John Richard was baptised at St Michael's Church on Spurriergate in York in 1827 but he must have died before our John Kendall was born. He was baptised on 13 May 1830 at St Olave in York. Frances, born in 1811, was the daughter of Richard Hobson MD, a practicing physician in Leeds, trained at Queens' College, Cambridge; he also had connections in York.

We know Frederick kept his interest in geology because H S Torrens tells of two articles he had published in John

Phillips' 'Illustrations of the Geology of Yorkshire' one in 1829 and the other in 1836, after his death. He was buried in Scarborough but his memorial is in Stonegrave. From the text on this memorial, erected by his widow and only son, we learn something of his character:

'his superior attainments and amiable disposition acquired for him the esteem and respect of an extensive circle of relatives and friends'

> SACRED TO THE MEMORY OF
> THE REV? FREDERICK KENDALL, B.A.,
> OF SIDNEY SUSSEX COLLEGE, CAMBRIDGE,
> 'VICAR OF RICCALL,
> AND A MAGISTRATE FOR
> THE EAST RIDING OF THIS COUNTY,
> ONLY SURVIVING SON OF
> THE LATE ADMIRAL JOHN KENDALL, OF SCARBOROUGH,
> HE DEPARTED THIS LIFE FEBRUARY THE 16 T.H 1836,
> IN THE 45 T.H YEAR OF HIS AGE.
> HIS SUPERIOR ATTAINMENTS
> AND AMIABLE DISPOSITION ACQUIRED FOR HIM
> THE ESTEEM AND RESPECT OF AN EXTENSIVE CIRCLE
> OF RELATIVES AND FRIENDS.
> THIS TABLET
> IS ERECTED BY HIS AFFECTIONATE RELICT,
> WHO WITH AN ONLY SON, IS LEFT TO SUSTAIN HIS LOSS.

The Spofforth Connection

What happened to the young widow and her six year old son left in the Vicarage in Riccall? Frances found a new husband in Edward Spofforth, born in 1811, son of Revd Ralph Spofforth, the Vicar of Howden. They married in 1837 and set up house in Riccall where their first two children, Richard and Fanny, were born. They had moved to Ferry House, Bishopthorpe, not far from the Archbishop's Palace, when Helen, Mary and Edward were born. John Kendall, now designated 'stepson' and 'landed proprietor', was living with them on both the 1851 and 1861 censuses. We have at last discovered where he spent his childhood. When Frances' second husband, Edward, died in 1861, they moved to 19 St Mary's Gate in Bootham. Frances herself died in York in 1887 at the age of 76.

The Spofforths were a well established family; this particular branch came from Howden according to Captain Ralph Spofforth in his detailed work 'A New History of the Spofforth Family'. John Kendall's youngest half-brother, Edward, born in Bishopthorpe in 1849, was a clerk with the Yorkshire Insurance Company, he married Mary Darley Fligg in 1886, which reconnected them to Scarborough.

The Fliggs were yet another ship-owning family. Her grandfather, William Fligg, had been a Trustee of Trinity House and Seamen's Hospital with William and Richard Mosey and William Tindall. Mary was the daughter of his son, also called William, and his wife Susannah. Her father had had the barque 'Isabel' built in 1857, named after his mother. The family moved from Castle Gate to the developing area of Falsgrave, their address on the 1861 census was number 4 West Parade where they were still living in 1881.

From the 1891 census we find that Edward and Mary Spofforth went to live in Grosvenor Terrace in York, with their two children, Frances Mary born in 1889 and Edward Reginald, born 15 June 1891. This is the elusive Frances Mary Spofforth who was a trustee from the first meeting of the John Kendall Trust in 1942. Her father died on 30 November 1891, less than six months after the birth of her brother Edward.

Mary Spofforth returned to her family in Scarborough, we find her on the 1901 census living at 17 Westbourne Grove with Frances aged 11, Edward 9, their grandmother, Suzannah, who had reached the age of 89, a resident domestic servant and a sick-nurse. Edward was sent to school at Giggleswick and later to Oundle. In 1911 he is recorded as being a clerk for the Yorkshire Insurance Company, working at William Drawbridge's office. When the war intervened he would have been 23, he answered the call and joined the Yorkshire Regiment in 1914. He held the rank of Lieutenant when he was killed at Sanctuary Wood near Ypres on 3 March 1916: he was buried in Poperinge. Edward's name is commemorated on the Fligg Family tombstone in Dean Road Cemetery, on Sir Tatton Sykes' Sledmere Cross, on the Scarborough Cenotaph at Oliver's Mount and in the Oundle Memorial Book.

Frances played her part in the First World War volunteering as a nurse in the Voluntary Aid Detachment. She remained in Scarborough giving her address as 9 Granville Road when updating Captain Ralph Spofforth on the family details, although from the John Kendall Trust Minute Book she was living at 15 Avenue Victoria in 1942. It is interesting to note that each of these addresses is quite close to West Street where her half-uncle, John Kendall, lived. Mary Darley Spofforth died in 1923, the same year as her half-brother-in-law John Kendall. As Frances had been named after John's mother, perhaps there was a close family bond?

It may have been John Kendall's wish that Frances should keep an eye on his legacy. Although she was not named in the Charity Commission Scheme of 1941, Miss F M Spofforth appeared on the typed list of the first Trustees in the Minute Book and may have been involved in the early days for which we have no records. Sydney McCloy and the other Trustees would have been aware of the family connection even though it took me a long time to work it out

The Trust met at the Alice Brooke Home but interest seemed to wane, after 1957 the meetings dropped to once a year. Miss Spofforth was re-elected every five years and served faithfully as a Trustee until her death on 13 May 1961. We find in the minutes of 11 December 1961:

'The late Miss F M Spofforth. It was unanimously agreed that the Trustees' appreciation of the

services so willingly rendered to the Trust be placed on record.'

The Trustees in attendance at that meeting were the Chairman, Canon D Oxby Parker, Miss L A Drew, Mr C H Bradley and Mr S D McCloy; apologies were received from Revd S Hankey: Miss E B Longbottom was elected to the committee in her place. Frances was still living at 15 Victoria Avenue when she died, leaving £100 in her will to the Alice Brooke Home.

Now what of Frederick's father, John Kendall's grandfather?

Rear-Admiral John Kendall

If you are looking for adventure, look no further. The John Kendall after whom our benefactor is named, was born in 1733 in the Nunnington area. His marriage to Ann Dowker on 27 July 1774 took place in St John's Church, Salton and Brawby, a parish adjoining Nunnington. John, whose occupation was given as Mariner, would have been 41 and Ann just 19. Their first child, Jane, married Edward Low in 1797, Captain in the Royal Irish Sensibles and it was their daughter, Sophia, who married our friend Samuel S Byron.

Their second daughter, Letitia, was born in 1783 and died in 1803, she is buried alongside her mother in St Mary's Churchyard in Scarborough; Ann died on 2 May 1809 aged 54. Two sons, John and James came next they were both baptised on 28 March 1787 but must have died young. 21 February 1788 saw the baptism of Marcia but no more is known of her and finally in 1790 we have their surviving son Frederick. All the baptisms took place in Stonegrave Church but Letitia had also had one a week earlier in Nunnington Church.

Ann's father, John, was probably a member of the Dowker family that from 1685 had provided that parish with its vicars over a period of 151 years. He may have been J

Dowker, Lord of the Manor in 1809, who died in 1816 and was succeeded by G W Dowker. British History on line tells us that in 1837 John Woodall bought the estate and passed it on to his son John Woodall Woodall. John W Woodall in turn left the property to his nephew C H Dent in 1905. Charles Henry was a brother of Mary Catherine Dent who was on the Scarborough School Board; he may have been the only one of the four sons to marry.

We transgress, back to John Kendall, Mariner. The middle of the 18th century was a lively time for the Navy. George III took the throne in 1760, in succession to his grandfather George II who had reigned since 1727. Admiral Anson was fighting the Spanish in the Caribbean and was also at the first Battle of Finisterre in 1747, part of the War of the Austrian Succession, 1740 – 1748. From 1756 to 1763 we have the Seven Years' War, also known as the French and Indian War; the Battle of Quebec was part of this when the Royal Navy supported General James Wolfe. During a peaceful period before 1775 when the American Revolutionary War began, nations took advantage, they explored the world in order to colonise new lands.

John Kendall, Mariner, was involved in most of these historical events. His notebooks were found as though someone was preparing to write his biography, from them we know that he sailed in the Channel Fleet in the Seven Years' War with John Byron on 'The Vanguard' in 1756, 'The America' in 1757 and 'The Fame' in 1760 helping to destroy the French fortifications in the Bay of Chaleur. In 1764 he was made 4th Officer on 'HMS Dolphin' under John Byron. This was a 24 gun, sixth rate, fully sailed frigate of the Royal Navy that had been launched in 1751: she was one of the first ships to be sheathed in copper and her rudder had copper braces and pintles.

John Byron, who was the grandfather of the poet Lord Byron, had sailed with Anson's fleet on a voyage of discovery in September 1740. He had met with disaster when the ship 'HMS Wager', under Captain Cheap, was wrecked after rounding Cape Horn. The crew mutinied but Cheap and Byron together with a few others reached the coast of Chile on 14 May 1741. They were badly treated but eventually made their way to Valparaiso and were rescued, returning home in 1745. Captain George Anson had continued his circumnavigation via China and Jakarta in 'The Centurion', his was the only ship from the original squadron of six to return home in July 1744.

Under the pretence of making a voyage to the East Indies 'The Dolphin', commanded by John Byron with John Kendall as 4th Officer, and 'The Tamar' under Captain Patrick Mouat, left the Downs outside Dover on 3 July 1764. Patrick Moat's son, Alexander, at the age of 15, accompanied Captain James Cook on his third voyage in the Whitby built ship 'Discovery' in 1776. Another member of the crew was Philip Carteret who was to captain his own ship, 'The Swallow', round the world in 1766. 'The Dolphin' and 'The Tamar' sailed via Funchal and the Cape Verde Islands but on reaching Rio they revealed to the crew that the true nature of their voyage was to explore the South Seas.

According to John Grimshaw's philatelic article on St Helena, George III had persuaded the Admiralty to search for the great continent that was believed to lie in the South Pacific; this was six years before Captain Cook landed in Botany Bay. James Cook's first voyage in this direction was not until 1769 when he tracked the transit of Venus from Tahiti in the famous bark 'Endeavour'. As far back as 1716 the astronomer Edmond Halley had calculated this event, which looks like a black disc crossing the sun. Cook's mission was to help in accurately setting the observer's longitude calculations, vital to the safety of the naval fleet.

The crews of the 'Dolphin' and the 'Tamar' were given the option of double pay or returning home, only one sailor disembarked. Their next port of call after Rio was on the hitherto unknown Saunders Island, part of the Falkland Islands which had already been visited by the French. There they gave the name Port Egmont, after the First Lord of the Admiralty, to the excellent harbour where they anchored. Having surveyed the islands, they took possession of them for Great Britain, leaving behind a flourishing vegetable garden. Byron was set on following Anson's earlier voyage as they sailed on, passing safely through the Magellan Straits.

Commodore John Byron landing in Patagonia in the Magellan Straits, HMS Dolphin and Tamar in the background – Friday 21st December 1764

Taking a course northwards across the Pacific Ocean, they came across a group of islands that were too rocky to make a landing on so they called them the Disappointment Islands. By this time their situation was becoming desperate as some of the sailors were suffering from scurvy and were in need of fresh supplies. From a lecture entitled 'Chronological list of the main maritime discoveries and explorations' printed in August 1944 in the International Hydrographic Review, Henri Bencker lists the places Byron visited. They include: the Danger Isles in the Prince of Wales Archipelago; the Land of King George and the Duke of York Island, otherwise known as Atafu or Tokelau, comprising a group of 42 coral islets in the middle of the

Pacific Ocean. They came across the Kingsmill Islands, also called the Gilbert Islands that are now known as Kiribati.

Byron made for Tinian, part of the Mariana Islands to the east of the Philippines, where they stayed for two months. The return home took them through Indonesia, via Jakarta, then known as Batavia, round the Cape of Good Hope to Table Bay, passing St Helena on Sunday 16 March 1766 without stopping. By reaching the Downs on 9 May 'The Dolphin' had made the fastest circumnavigation to date, taking twenty-two months and six days. 'The Tamar' had developed a problem and diverted to Antigua reaching home a month later.

John Kendall's adventures do not stop here. Between 1769 and 1778 he sailed on 'The Antelope', 'The Panther' and 'The Princess Royal'. He was made a Post Captain in 1778 when the American Revolutionary War was well underway, Independence had been declared on 4 July 1776. Captain Kendall was given command of his own ship a frigate 'The Rainbow' in 1779 with 350 men and 44 guns, she was a troopship on harbour service in American Coastal Waters. She was a known participant at the Siege of Charlestown in 1780 when Lt Gen Charles Lord Cornwallis assumed command of the British forces. It is probable that she took part in the Battle of Chesapeake Bay. In October 1781 Cornwallis surrendered to George Washington and the ships returned home; the Treaty of Paris was signed in 1783.

When John Kendall retired from the Navy he took up residence in Auborough Street, Scarborough. His superannuation as Rear-Admiral was granted on 3 July 1795. It is recorded in *'The Royal Kalendar, Or, Complete and Correct Annual Register for England, Scotland, Ireland and America'* dated 1817, that superannuated Rear Admirals received 25 shillings a day, John Kendall Esq. is included in the accompanying list. He died on 8 July 1824 and was buried at St Mary's Church two days later.

It is possible that Samuel Standidge Byron of West Ayton, at whose marriage to Sophie Lowe, granddaughter of Admiral Kendall, Revd Frederick Kendall officiated, was related to John Byron, Commander of 'The Dolphin' but I have not found the link.

Perhaps the reason for John Kendall's specific clause to support education *'on a Training Ship or at a Sea Training School'* when he drew up his Trust was due to his grandfather's illustrious career at sea. One might assume he would have inherited from the Rear-Admiral and perhaps he was the person who was going to write the biography. Here we pick up the connection between Revd Charles Edmund Swinnerton, erstwhile Vicar of St Thomas' Church, and Colonel John Kendall. Can it have been purely coincidental that Revd Swinnerton was chosen as a Trustee when he had spent four years in Jesselton (now Kota Kinabalu) in Borneo, a remote part of the world where John's Grandfather had sailed some two hundred years before?

The John Kendal Trust continues to help those who wish to go to sea by awarding grants to the Sea Cadet Corps. How appropriate that as recently as 2013, a Sea Cadet was enabled to take part as a buddy on the Jubilee Sailing Ship 'The Lord Nelson' in Australia. Similarly we have the Rainbow connection, a neat place to end this section on the John Kendall Trust as this charity has been pleased to support the Scarborough Rainbow Centre, St Mary's Church outreach into the community, working with families who find themselves in need in the 21st century.

***

In Conclusion

This has been a fascinating journey for me, and I hope for you too, discovering so many interesting people who contributed to these children's charities. When I set out I had some idea about some of the people involved and the way the charities operate today but I had not appreciated how intertwined the people and organisations actually were.

Across the years there are various threads like the Churches, government, sea-faring, tourism, the Charity Commission, newspapers and printing that weave their way through our history. Individual people, often going down the generations in a family, play their part in the life of the town. Through time they make things work well for the good of the community – yes, just like we continue to do today.

Copperplate may have given way to computers but the curiosity that drives people to venture into new realms and the compassion that urges them to improve things for other people is still alive and well. If we take the Rainbow Centre as an example, St Mary's Church continues to reach out to the community to support those in need. It is in turn supported by other churches and individuals in the community, almost like the Amicable Society was supported some three hundred years earlier. The Sea Cadet Corps performs a similar role to that of the Sea Training School in the past, encouraging young people to take up careers at sea, still supported by the John Kendall Trust.

Buildings that played a significant part in our story and would have been familiar to our ancestors serve as concrete reminders of our past, like the Castle, the Spa, the Cliff Bridge, the Rotunda, the Town Hall, our beautiful old churches, Paradise House and the Library to name but a few. I loved meeting new people, like Simpson Parkinson and Johnny Jackson, to find out what a difference a helping hand had made to their lives. Who knows what the young people we help at the moment will do in the future?

The two characters I found most surprising were William Ascough and Rear-Admiral John Kendall. William's personal journey was amazing then we find he was prepared to share his expertise to give others the same opportunities. John Kendall's real journey almost reaching Australia before Captain Cook was a revelation, why had I not heard about him before? To find the Story of Heming was another thrilling moment! For me Tostig had merely been a name on a sundial at St Gregory's Minster in Kirkdale, now we know he was brother to King Harold, with one sister married to Edward the Confessor and another sister may have lived in Scarborough.

Our forebears experienced the repercussions of many national events we read about in history books, like Richard Lionheart setting out on his Crusade, the ravages of the Civil Wars as well as the more recent conflicts. Our personal connections with St John Ambulance made the discovery that St Sepulchre Street was named after the Knights Templar returning from the Holy Land thought-provoking. I try to picture the Franciscan monks working on the same site that I did when at the Technical College some eight hundred years later. Thanks to their ingenuity the town's inhabitants were able to thrive because of the supply of fresh water: I had wondered how Scarborough could exist without having a river.

To have been a fly on the wall at the meetings of the Education Committee would have been interesting especially when you think William Ascough was trying to set up a system that bears a close resemblance to today's Comprehensive Education when they clashed with County Hall over the 'Muni' in 1900. There are so many echoes of present day debates on educational ideology; will we ever get it right?

Some parts of the story were like unravelling string; the Rowntree family for example, the Woodalls and the local government systems, working out who belonged where and who did what. There had to be a reason why various things happened the way they did so I felt I needed to look at the relevant Acts of Parliament; a bit dry perhaps but we see the outcomes translated into the evolution of our school system.

I was surprised to discover how many eminent people came to live here, often in retirement, and were willing to share their expertise like Revd James Acworth and Sir Arthur Dyke Acland, the retired Education Minister who had been responsible for some of the legislation. Scarborough was not as 'stuck-in-the-mud' as I had thought, people kept up-to-date with the ideas of the time. Conversely many Scarborough people spread their influence all over the world, like Frederick Mosey and William Hewitt who settled in far flung places.

In essence, little has changed. Our churches continue to work together, laying aside their differences. Our MPs, Borough and County Councillors keep trying to make good decisions, not always appreciated by all the people. Today's society is still as generous with time and money as in the past, sometimes needing a little encouragement or chivvying. Although the Welfare State has been with us for many years, charitable organisations are still vital, which is why these three children's charities, their original constitutions slightly amended to suit current needs, continue to operate today.

The Amicable Society still provides school uniforms, footwear and a friendly warden to advise families who find themselves in hard times. Local companies still help with hampers of goodies and vouchers at Christmas. SUSF is called upon by students from primary school through to university level, who are in need of grants towards educationally related expenses. These can include field trips, particular equipment for studying at college or university, very often technology related, or for starting work, virtually on the same lines that William Ascough set up in 1888. The John Kendall Trust, whilst supporting individual children whose families are on benefits or who may have special educational needs, also offers help to organisations designed to enhance the life-opportunities of young people in difficult circumstances. The Charity Commission has recently given permission for it to include young people up to the age of 25, in line with SUSF guidelines.

We hope these benefactors from the past would approve of what we are doing in the present day world. We are grateful to them for the way their generosity and foresight continues to give encouragement to today's children.

****